The Art of Decision Making

THE ART OF DECISION MAKING

MAKING

ISSUES AND CASES IN HIGHER EDUCATION

Patricia R. Plante

American Council on Education • Macmillan Publishing Company
NEW YORK

Collier Macmillan Publishers
LONDON

Macmillan Publishing Company
866 Third Avenue, New York, N.Y. 10022

Collier Macmillan Canada, Inc.

Library of Congress Catalog Card Number: 86-28443

Printed in the United States of America

printing number
1   2   3   4   5   6   7   8   9   10

Library of Congress Cataloging in Publication Data

Plante, Patricia R.
   The art of decision making.

   (American Council on Education/Macmillan series on
higher education)
   Bibliography: p.
   Includes index.
   1. Universities and colleges—United States—Administra-
tion. 2. Decision-making. I. Title. II. Series:
American Council on Education/Macmillan series in
higher education.
LB2341.P57   1987   378.73   86-28443
ISBN 0-02-924550-8

"Despina can be reached in two ways: by ship or by camel. The city displays one face to the traveler arriving overland and a different one to him who arrives by sea."

Italo Calvino
Invisible Cities

Contents

Preface

The purpose of this work is to share with fellow academic administrators and with those who aspire to replace us imagined experiences in decision making. Recent studies by cognitive psychologists such as David McClelland at Harvard, Ulric Neisser at Emory, and Siegfried Streufert at Penn State College of Medicine point to the complexity of decision making, the practical intelligence most effective in reaching conclusions, and the tacit, hence difficult to articulate and to transmit, quality of mind that makes for sound judgments. Virtually every decision is multidimensional and the ability to see the multiple connections involved is more of an art than a science.

However, while it is true that there is an element in every administrative decision that, like a poem, defies analysis, living through many experiences that force one to arrive at solutions to complex cases does help the talented to develop the art of leadership. "Living through" the management experiences in order to hone one's art is time-consuming, dangerous, and necessary. However, to "live through" similar and common experiences in a vicarious manner is fast, safe, and equally important. Though poems should speak as directly as an idiom, most of us must spend years dissecting them before reaching a level of expertise where our understanding of them is immediate. Likewise, though wise and fair resolutions to complex human problems should come immediately to the mind of an academic administrator, most of us must spend years dissecting all the elements in hundreds of cases before we have perfected the art form called administration. This book's purpose is to allow the reader, in the time it takes to read it and to think about it, to live through years of direct experience vicariously. Obviously, to read about walking along rue St. Honoré in Paris is not to walk along rue St. Honoré. However, such reading can imaginatively prepare you for walking it; remind you of what it was like to walk it; point out details you may have missed and that you should look for the next time you walk it.

Since most of us share a healthy curiosity about one another's professional lives, and since that curiosity is probably, at least in part, derived from our appetite for stories, the structure of this book attempts to take advantage of this natural bent by using case studies as a catalyst for thought about administrative principles. Each case study deals with an issue that is both significant and perennial, such as sexual harassment, alleged discrimination, intercollegiate athletics and academic integrity, and disturbances and dissent. These cases are sandwiched between an opening chapter that describes the values that inform the work and a concluding one that suggests what to look for in choosing decision makers.

Each case study contains:

1. A brief description of an issue that often confronts administrators, for example, academic freedom, relationship with the outside community, inventory control
2. The background of a particular case, that is, conditions that might affect a managerial decision
3. The happening, that is, the actual problem and the factors that precipitated it
4. A suggested course of action including options with attendant possible consequences

In each case, a solution is "suggested" not because the tone of the book is tentative, but because resolutions to most administrative problems are not right or wrong, but wise or unwise. The book recognizes throughout that every decision made by an administrator reveals his values and should, if wise, take into consideration a campus's culture. Each suggested course of action includes the principles, both philosophical and managerial, that led to the proposed conclusion, and each is intended to promote discussion and possibly to raise controversy. The book follows this rather rigid pattern throughout so as to afford the reader the opportunity to solve each case himself by facing an imagined situation that requires immediate action. The intent is thereby to maintain interest and tension by postponing temporarily and at the reader's option the ending of the "story." A number of notices:

1. Distracting and upon occasion irrelevant subplots have been introduced in several cases because problems often enter one's professional life bearing false passports.
2. Several of the suggested solutions to problems are intended to be provocative but none are less than serious and all are in

keeping with the values described in the opening and closing chapters, which attempt to convey a commitment to unambiguous points of view.

3. The number of details given in each case could not have been exhaustive without turning each case into a full-length work. The reader can, however, change each story and consequently its ending by simply varying the conditions or the characters by certain degrees or by adding information that has not been provided.

4. While this book is not intended to suggest that experience is a substitute for theory nor to devalue the need all administrators have for a basic knowledge of management science and a history of higher education, it does insist that a training in financial abstractions, computer modeling, and strategic planning, however useful, is no guarantee whatever of either effective academic leadership or of sound management. And it further insists that management of colleges/universities might profitably be taught as an interdisciplinary program in the humanities.

5. In all instances the cases are works of fiction. The institutions and characters while intended as plausible are imaginary and the stories in which they appear have been invented, not re-created.

6. Both men and women appear as administrators in all of the case studies. When upon occasion the masculine pronoun is used in generalizations, no gender is specified or intended. The pronoun is used generically.

7. This book attempts above all to avoid dullness and safety.

South Portland, Maine Patricia R. Plante
April 1986

Acknowledgments

Portions of Chapter One have appeared in *Liberal Education* and *The Chronicle of Higher Education* and are reprinted here with the permission of these publications.

A section of Chapter One and Chapter Fourteen has appeared in different form in *Change* ("The Attack on Tenure: the Threat from Within," November/December, 1983, pp. 10–11 and "Educational Authenticity," January/February, 1986, pp. 8–9). *Change* is a publication of the Helen Dwight Reid Educational Foundation.

I am deeply grateful to my secretary, Sue Ann Nordhoff, who prepared the manuscript of this work and who has lived through many an academic crisis with admirable aplomb.

The Art of Decision Making

CHAPTER ONE
VISIONS AND DECISIONS

Decision making in academe is no less value free than decision making elsewhere, nor should it be. Consequently, administrators driven by dissimilar convictions and inspired by different visions may arrive quite legitimately at varied solutions to the same problem. All well and good, for a college/university's culture is formed in significant part by a system of shared values, which an administrator should help form, should periodically question, and should consistently support. The great danger lies not in administrators on all 3,000-odd American campuses pursuing sundry ideals and promoting varied convictions, but in administrators pursuing and promoting nothing but a peace and a harmony that often accompanies mediocrity.

The suggested courses of action to the miniature dramas in subsequent chapters are both framed and colored by the three tenets of faith that follow, for, ultimately, all decisions regarding serious matters transcend management techniques. While those in power may not have reached consensus on how to define leadership, most are now persuaded that no one exercises it without aim and without fixed beliefs.

1. An academic administrator must lead a vigorous intellectual life.

The adoption of any number of management styles can lead to success in academic administration, providing one carefully seeks a glove-perfect fit between the chosen style and one's own personality. However, regardless of style, the cultivation of one habit is de rigueur. Once a semester, every academic dean and vice-president must make two statements: one, "I miss teaching and wish I had time to do more of it," and two, "I'm busier than you can image. This semester is the busiest ever." This state of an administrator's life need not be described in a formal address. A dean might, for example, be overheard referring to this condition at a reception following the year's opening convocation, or may even confide this malaise to the prominent faculty gossip in the privacy of his office. The important thing is to send the message and to be sure that it is received.

Now, to express a desire to return to the classroom if only one could, is not only harmless, but touchingly human for a number of reasons. It is an admission, however oblique, that teaching, in all its forms, and not management, in any form, is the central mission of a college/university. It is a confession, however unconscious, that the changing of one's mind, even if now socially acceptable, was at one time probably the only sin upon which everyone could agree. And, finally, it is a sign, however dim, that even in midlife one needs to cling to illusions, for many who express this wish could make it come true if they really wanted to.

However, the second of the two statements, namely, that each term is busier than the previous one, is a far more serious matter, for it may mask a dangerous ordering of priorities that could ultimately weaken an administrator's capacity to provide intellectual leadership.

While the life of contemplation can never, of necessity, be central to that of an administrator's days, the temptation to avoid it altogether is as alluring as it is perilous. To read an intellectually demanding book, to think through a difficult problem, to write a thoughtful essay requires greater psychic energy than does discussing strategies with the marketing team, or reviewing the long-range office automation plan, or dictating a memo explaining the denial of a request for funds. And if one runs out of routine matters, one can always find a crisis in the chemistry department where a vacuum pump is malfunctioning or in the Financial Aid Office where the director will be pleased to spend any amount of time discussing the inadequacies of the Finance Division. And at the end of any average 50/60-hour week, one can point to a long list of activities that will justify one's gasping for breath.

But after the conferences, after the meetings, after the memos, after all that and so much more, what directions has the busy administrator given the university? What values have been supported? What inspiration has been provided? Has the winded dean stepped off the treadmill even long enough to ask the questions let alone to answer them?

To confront this hardworking and well-meaning academic officer is not in any way to suggest that financial aid officers should not be heard, that contractors who disrupt chemistry laboratory sessions by installing defective vacuum pumps should not be made aware of the error of their ways, or that all or even many memos are unnecessary. It is to say, however, that without time devoted to study and reflection, the decisions made and the actions taken may eventually lack inner consistency, and that the judgment calls may in time be in serious need of corrected vision.

One of the threats in the professional life of an academic administrator is identical to one of the threats in life itself, namely, everydayness. After having spent virtually all of one's adult life absorbing the characteristics of academe's culture, and after having spent a number of years as a dean and/or vice-president, one can predict with notable accuracy the response of a department, the conclusions of an investigative committee, or the nature of students' complaints under specific circumstances. Such acclimatization can, of course, result in impressive efficiency, for many responses to problems are, under such conditions, mechanical. And therein lies the danger: All responses may with time become mechanical. Premises may never be reexamined and creative solutions to recurring problems may never be discovered. This condition is the administrator's version of the professor's yellow-with-age lecture notes syndrome.

Colleges/universities are amazingly resilient institutions that can survive for years under mechanical administrators, for good machines do have a number of characteristics that are valuable, even if efficiency is not the queen of virtues. Here is one of Max Frisch's fictional characters praising the qualities of the robot as described in *Homo Faber:*

> Above all, however, the machine has no feelings, it feels no fear and no hope, which only disturb, it has no wishes with regard to the result, it operates according to the pure logic of probability. For this reason I assert that the robot perceives more accurately than man, it knows more about the future, for it calculates it, it neither speculates nor dreams, but is controlled by its own findings (the feedback) and cannot make mistakes; the robot has no need of intuition . . . (Harvest/Harcourt Brace Jovanovich, New York, 1959, p. 76).

However, a college/university governed by academic robots will discover over time that while it is not plagued by law suits, while registration runs smoothly, while faculty meet their classes and students attend them, its spirit has died. It will discover that while it feels no fear, it feels no hope, and that while dreams are no substitute for logic, logic is no substitute for dreams.

A college/university is its faculty. But a modern-day faculty with its many specializations and its multiple responsibilities need as never before to feel part of a whole, and need to be certain that the whole knows where it is going and why. That sense of direction and of purpose must come from its academic administrators, who, if not inspired themselves, cannot inspire others. Robots, for all their efficiency and reliability, cannot promote a sense of being intensely alive. And "alive" in academe means "intellectually alive." Hence, academic administrators have as their primary responsibility the continual cultivation of their own intellectual life so as to fulfill their obligation of providing ever-renewed enthusiasm for any college/university's central conviction: that an intellectually rich life is to be preferred to an intellectually impoverished one.

Fulfilling this primary responsibility may be, of all responsibilities, the most challenging for any administrator for two reasons. First, everydayness is Everyman's enemy, and academic administrators cannot be expected to transcend the human condition. We all spend our lives in combat against a foe that would have us settle for the little pleasures: a good glass of Chablis and daydreams before an open fire. Eugene Ionesco in his autobiographical work, *Present Past, Past Present*, reminds us of the brilliance of color before habit places a veil before our eyes. When a child, he takes a walk along a little hillside.

> I cross a sunken path, full of shadows, and come out in full sunlight; red poppies in yellow wheat, a blue, blue sky. I have never again seen a red that bright, a yellow that yellow, a blue as intense, a light as yellow, as fresh, as new. It must have been the first day of creation. The world had just been created and everything was untouched. Everything has since gotten tired, all the colors have faded, habit has cast a shadow over all that. Our eyes have grown tired from so much light; we have lost paradise (Grove Press, Inc., New York, 1971, p. 25).

A yearly assault of 700 meetings, 3,000 memos, 4,000 telephone calls, and, now, the threat of finding messages on the IBM PC screen, all related to perennial academic problems and demanding decisions, can eventually color every day a uniform gray. A second reason for the challenge is that academic administrators, in an attempt to meet all the responsibilities found in their typical job descriptions, truly are as busy as they say they are. They do in fact put in 60-hour weeks.

Consequently, the temptation is to avoid both challenges: to live with a blurred vision and to spend so much time and energy on the second and the fourteenth and the twenty-fifth responsibility that the first one, providing intellectual leadership, is given less and less emphasis, until, finally, one is no longer capable of meeting that obligation. At that hour, one has settled, both as a person and as an administrator for what Walker Percy has called "the Little Way." One has abandoned the big search for the intensely alive experiences and settled for the dim, little pleasures of efficiently run offices. Not to meet the first challenge is a betrayal of the self; not to meet the second, in part as a consequence of not having met the first, is a betrayal of the institution.

There is but one defense against such betrayals: an energetic life of the mind throughout one's professional life as an administrator. Not "an energetic life of the mind" some afternoon if there is no practical problem to solve, no faculty to see, no enrollment statistics to check. Not "an energetic life of the mind" as in the exchange of experiences with colleagues over lunch or as in the reading of the "Higher Education Daily." But "an energetic life of the mind" as in the rereading of Aristotle, Cellini, and Proust.

If we believe that a study of the liberal arts provides insight and perspective, then we should live as if we believed it, and our administrative decisions should be informed by the serious examination of the view of philosophers, critics, and scientists. If cultural happenings are an important component of a civilized world, then we should behave as if we meant that. We should attend concerts and see films and spend time in museums.

Wilfrid Sheed, in remarks delivered at Southampton College of Long Island University and reprinted in the *New York Times* in June 1980, said that "the professional world becomes a kind of Franz Kafka mansion where the rooms get spiritually smaller and grayer the further up the stairs you go, and this is known as promotion." The way to dispel this spiritual darkness and gloom, is to be sure that our minds match our offices: with each promotion they should become better and better furnished.

2. An academic administrator must not adopt a style that is inimical to the distinctive nature of a college/university.

Your mother may never have read Pascal, who in his *Pensées* claims that "all men's misfortunes spring from the single cause that they are unable to stay quietly in one room." She did, however, perhaps often admonish you to sit still, and you may have come to appreciate the advice and to conclude that all administrators should, at least upon occasion, consider its wisdom.

The most glaring sign of anxiety inspired by declining enrollments and accompanying fiscal constraints in higher education is a frenzied social and political activity on the part of its administrators that is difficult to distinguish from that customarily expected of heads of real-estate firms and automobile dealerships. For while presidents of colleges/universities and, to a lesser extent, vice-presidents and deans, have always been looked upon as community leaders who now and then graced a dais at ceremonial functions, it was generally accepted as a given that their domain was not quite of this world, that, somehow, they were above the daily fray and that the leadership they could be expected to provide was intellectual. In a word, it was nice of them to have come, but even nicer of them to have left early so that the party could really get started. And what everyone assumed they did after they had left was to go home to read and to think. Not as exciting a function in life as that of selling Alfa Romeos, even dull perhaps, but honorable, and certainly to be respected—if only at a comfortable distance.

However, now that college/university administrators have become CEOs, to think is to sleep. They either make the Sunday edition or they head that somnambulant little (or big) place in the heart of the city or in the western part of the county. Their effectiveness as academic leaders is more and more frequently measured in the community by the number of times they are seen in the "People" section of newspapers and how often they are featured as "People to Watch." It is a phenomenon somewhat reminiscent of your eighth-grade's mimeographed monthly containing articles on the class officers' favorite foods. Even the *Chronicle of Higher Education* has caught the fever and surveys selected presidents to see what books they plan to read in the summer—as if reading were a recreational activity like snorkeling. Now, one could dismiss the matter as "great fun, but just one of those things" if some faculty on many campuses had not, in their own brand of anxiety, begun to sympathize with that world view. Professors who, even 5 years ago, expressed an aristocratic disdain for administrators who sought the goodwill of those who pay homage to publicity-seekers are now heard complaining that the president is not "out there making the important contacts."

Ironically, until fairly recently, 20/30 years or so, the college/ university administrator as businessman/woman and promoter of hype who was engaged in establishing contacts was the subject of derision and mistrust if not outright animosity in the academic community. The European notion of "trade" as being beneath those who were educated/cultured had influenced not only higher education, but secondary schools (especially private ones) into viewing business in all its varied styles as possibly proper for those who could not master literary studies. Just as one was brought up never to refer in public to the cost of anything, so too one grew up in schools that shunted indifferent learners into "commercial courses" and colleges/universities that relegated the subject of business to the rank of parvenue among the elite disciplines.

However, the complexities of managing growth in the 1960s and 1970s and of managing decline in the 1980s have, among other factors, altered this attitude dramatically in both governing boards and departments of linguistics. Indeed, some institutional groups, no wiser though less snobbish than their forebears, now see the marketing expert as the fountain of grace and the effective ad- ministrator of a university as a clever, energetic, and sociable mar- keting expert.

In this altered culture, "a good man/woman" is one who smiles broadly, shakes hands firmly, and speaks warmly. While a good man/woman will, upon every permissible occasion, become serious and discuss higher education, he/she limits the subject to the health of the market: enrollment figures and state/federal funding on the big board; office automation and intercollegiate athletics on the over-the-counter board. Of course, a good man/ woman is interested in the question of the knowledge most worth having, in the consequences of a significant decline of enrollment in the humanities, in the inadequate preparation of those who aspire to teach others, in intellectually undemanding curricula that place a nation at risk, in all of these crucial issues and in so many others of equal importance. However, how are good persons ex- pected to read and to think and to write about matters that are at the heart of their enterprise? After all, a university is "big busi- ness" and they are already working 15 hours a day "pressing flesh" and "getting ink."

While some administrators seem unwilling or unable to tran- scend the incipient postulates of the times, while some faculty seem to have come to expect the administrators of their institutions to appropriate the style of business and public relations executives, many students have become aware of the price/earning ratios of the various possible investments of self. "College Freshmen Aspire to Wealth Rather Than A Meaningful Life" reads a headline of the *Higher Education Daily*. "Life is now," and not "now" in a philosophy or a history of science course, but "now" in an internship with the local real-estate firm where networking may begin. They have been told in many ways and have learned well not to sit still, but to study on the run; to keep one part of the mind on the text, but the other in constant readiness to spy the opportunity. You meet them in their dark suits and club ties, already looking over your shoulder at receptions, ever poised to pounce upon the meta-contact, or, in a phrase of the times, the "quality contact." They are "good young men/women" who are being cheated by colleges/universities that all too often have failed to establish a climate that should develop in them a need—an absolute need—for contemplation; for a wish to watch from the sidelines long enough to return to the game with insight; for a desire to examine the questions surrounding being and becoming and to understand how Hindus as opposed to Christians or Jews or Muslims have attempted to answer them through time; for not being embarrassed or bored by matters of literary or philosophical or artistic seriousness.

In unguarded moments, students of all persuasions, even those who move too quickly to elect courses in the arts and sciences, show signs of knowing on some level that hype may be more appropriate to selling rock albums than colleges/universities. We have all witnessed an 18 year old treat a glossy brochure from campus X or Y with the same respect and interest as he bestows upon a Wisconsin cheese catalogue. And now from Jan Krukowski Associates, Inc. of New York come the results of a recent study showing that advertising by colleges not only fails to recruit students, but actually "has immeasurable negative effects on overall perceptions of the quality of the institution that advertises." According to the management newsletter, *Administrator*, surveys conducted in the fall of 1983 showed that between 56 and 61% of students with combined SATs of at least 1,000 reported that advertising detracted from a school's stature.

In the past 20 years, the culture of the world of business has had a significant influence upon the culture of the world of academe. A long and thoughtful study is needed to determine whether management by objectives, MBO, should have been left to General Motors and Theory Z to Hewlett Packard, but an empirical knowledge of the changes in decision making wrought by this influence would suggest that colleges/universities may have lost at least as much as they have gained by adopting what were once alien mores. Just as academe in the late 1960s may have been far too docile in accepting, even welcoming, flagellation at the hands of those who called for revolutionary changes, so too colleges/universities in the late 1970s and the 1980s may be seen by future historians as once more having been far too long on action and far too short on thought in embracing the ways, means, and style of business enterprises and their chief officers. What is good for General Motors is not necessarily good for a university.

We continue to read articles on the new breed of academic administrators: CEOs who manage by objectives, establish marketing teams, and do not view the jargon of long-range planning as linguistic adventures in academe. However, while the times undoubtedly call for the use of some of the techniques of the marketplace, and while these techniques may indeed, as some claim, make us leaner and stronger, they should come with four warning labels.

One, the business model has always placed a great emphasis on the appearance of success: on the size of offices and the thickness of the pile in the carpet. And one could point out that the more we insist on describing universities/colleges as, after all, business enterprises, the more emphasis accrediting teams place on the physical plant and the more young administrators want the office furniture and wallpaper in coordinated colors. For example, a university in the East was recently criticized by an accrediting team evaluating its dance program for not providing a larger office for the director of the program and an attached or nearby reasonably sized room to accommodate meetings with her faculty. Now, without being of the art in the garret school, it is valuable to remind ourselves that there is no necessary correlation between creativity and the view from an office window. A very fine dean calls one day and asks, "Do you know that the maintenance department has push-button phones?" Well, no, you guess you did not know that. "Do you have push-button phones?" You have to look, but, sure enough, your phone is the old-fashioned dial kind. What is going on here? The person who mows the lawn has a push-button phone, and the chief academic officer of the university has to wait for the dial to turn? What kind of system of values do we have? It is only a short illogical leap from this to "The president is an antiintellectual who does not care about the academic, so what can you expect."

Even the poorest among our institutions can hardly be described as ascetic, and while one need not recommend that faculty write manuscripts in unheated cells and that students eat their meals in monastic refectories, it is essential to reexamine the details of our professional lives and the values that inform our decisions often enough to be able to defend them in the light of our mission.

Two, while American businesses, as opposed to foreign ones, are now being criticized for being absorbed with the short view of quarterly earnings at the expense of the long view of progress, it is nevertheless true that a *carpe diem* philosophy is of necessity at the core of any business's profitable strategic planning. Hence, the harmless, albeit at times tacky, hype in a world where timing and goodwill is everything. However, the moment may be the very thing a university should not seize, for one of its values to society and one of its very reasons for being is to take the long and complex view when all other institutions, be they economic or political or religious or social, are too busy or too involved to do so. Universities have as part of their mission the obligation to place events and points of view within the context of man's long intellectual history and to expose both to the light of man's best thinking. Therefore, a college/university and its administrators must maintain a distance that will allow them to be engaged with contemporary happenings only to the extent that will not interfere with the quiet and leisure and meditative climate necessary to study with objectivity and to reflect with dispassion. It is hype at its worst to try to persuade the American public that in answer to some perceived need the university has transformed its Jamesian observers into George F. Babbitts.

Three, yet another danger in adopting the business model is that the administrator of a university who spends time and energy trying to persuade the members of the business community that he also is one of them—that his profession does not differ from theirs, may actually succeed. While we must, of course, manage efficiently and manage creatively, our institutions differ dramatically from business enterprises. We do not manage well for profit; we manage well in order to be able to continue doing something that is primarily profitable to the spirit and mind of man. If other benefits accrue, all well and good, but they are not of the essence.

And to the extent that an administrator does not maintain the image of an intellectual leader as opposed to someone who "produces" medical technicians and sociologists, the community will forget the mission of a university and think of it as simply one more institution that deals in commodities. We must be very careful about the mask we decide to wear; for after a while, we cannot take it off. We have become the image we worked so long to create.

Managing and decision making in a period of decline is far more complex than managing and decision making in a period of growth, for there is no money in the budget to pay for the vines that would hide the cracks. No wonder many dream of a world where running from legislative breakfasts, to alumni luncheons, to dinners for benefactors would somehow eliminate the need to arrive at well-reasoned, thoughtful positions regarding the value of tenure, the humanities, and the core curriculum. Such well-intentioned vigorous activity is attractive above all for its simplicity: I break bread with everybody; everybody breaks bread with me; and, as a result, the faculty, the staff, and the students eat. The clean, minimal look of such a premise, however reduced to its basic element, is in elegant contrast to the rococo style that characterizes, of necessity, the solutions to so many problems confronting administrators. Hence, its nearly irresistible appeal. And when life becomes too much like a pathless wood, we can forgive a poet for becoming a swinger of birch trees, I suppose we should at least sympathize with those who seek nice, clean lines. However, the world is too much with us; simplicity will not do.

A fourth, and probably not final, danger to be sensitive to in academe's rapprochement with business is the commercialization of the professoriat. Observers of contemporary trends have drawn our attention to the effects of the profit motive among professionals in medicine and law. The age of high technology with its concomitant commercialism has transformed the health profession to the point where to speak of becoming a physician as a matter of high calling seems touching and quaint. And to imagine lawyers struggling with the ethics of comparative sciences and philosophies of law becomes increasingly difficult when local attorneys advertise their services much in the same manner as do the managers of Pizza Huts. Now, while no one institution ever completely outstrides the weaknesses of its age, colleges/universities are measured by the degree to which they succeed. That in essence means by the degree to which their administrators and faculty succeed. And if an institution of higher learning is primarily a business, then the rewards for its employees should be the same as the rewards for those who sell more and better telephones: money and bonus trips to Martinique in January. Already the professor/consultant is too disengaged from his vocation to teach freshmen, to advise undergraduates, to carry a fair share of the burdens of shared governance, and, above all, to maintain the distance necessary for insightful and scholarly observation. And, who will remind him of the excess of his ways? Who will set the tone for a community of learners? The administrator as business executive?

Good management and appropriate leadership in a university demand, above all, that we always, but especially in times of fiscal constraint, keep our minds, our energies, and our resources directed toward the accomplishment of our distinctive mission. That means avoiding byroads however attractive or however worthy of travel. A college/university is not a day-care center, a gerontology complex, a legislative arena, a settlement house, a high-tech industry, a church, a sports stadium. It is not even a business. It is, to borrow Jacques Barzun's lovely phrase, "a house of intellect" where one learns to deal with abstract thought primarily, though not exclusively, through books. An attempt to be anything else, a decision to appropriate a style in keeping with anything else, will scatter our resources, confuse our communities, demoralize our dedicated faculties, and cheat our serious students.

3. An academic administrator must understand and protect the central role of the faculty in a college/ university.

At the 1981 ceremony in which the novelist Marguerite Yourcenar was admitted to the French Academy, the immortals, the artists, sat on a dais situated above that of Giscard D'Estaing, then president of the Republic. Now, admittedly, the French newspapers were quick to point out, Monsieur le Président sat on a Louis XV fauteuil, but, nevertheless, it was placed on a level *below* that of Yourcenar and that of her colleagues—as, indeed, it should have been. Politics come and go, as poor Giscard was soon to discover, but art remains. When King Tut's tomb was opened, no one searched for a copy of the king's policies and procedures, but everyone was awed by that golden mask. Even a pope, whose name we forget, is forgiven certain indiscretions because he had the good taste to support Benvenuto Cellini.

The Yourcenar anecdote is illustrative. Without false modesty, without pious references to the etymology of the word "administer" from the Latin, "administrare" meaning to serve, successful administrators do not allow themselves to forget that while they may sit at the head table, the quality of the banquet, however they assess quality, depends on the faculty.

Nearly every academician of a certain age will recall a time when the space occupied by administrative offices on campus was half its present size and when no self-respecting scholar would have spent time reading directives and policies from those who somehow kept the radiators hot in winter. Those were the days preceding "environmental scanning models," the days before we generated enough paperwork to fill floor after floor of our campus glass towers in tribute to the American conviction that bigger is better. And while some of this managerial frenzy is necessary and some even beneficial, no one should be deluded into thinking, even for an unguarded moment, that there is where the university's heart beats. Of course, a university without administrative leadership will falter and may even lose its way. Of course, an institution of higher education will be judged in part by its support services. However, after you have searched for excellence, after you have analyzed the megatrends, after you have hired your one-minute managers, after you have discussed both Theory Z and Theory Y, after all of this and so much more, the university is its faculty. The university is that one integrative mind sharing what is known and seeking what is unknown in lecture halls and seminar rooms and libraries and laboratories. An academic administrator forgets this not only at his own peril, but at the peril of his institution.

This conviction influences decision making in a great many areas, but may exert the most power in matters dealing with faculty development and tenure. Once an administrator is convinced that in truth the faculty is the college/university, it follows that the nurturing of faculty talent must head any priority list. Generous funds, however tight the budget, are then directed toward providing a faculty every possible opportunity for self-renewal and intellectual development.

It is a very rare instance, indeed, when what is good for faculty development is not good for the college/university. Consequently, an academic administrator should support with creativity and enthusiasm sabbaticals and leaves of absence for research; should provide institutional grants for scholarship and improvement of teaching; should budget for reduced teaching loads to allow the completion of a book or of a musical composition; should pay registration fees at professional meetings; should finance travel connected with the reading of scholarly papers; should encourage invitations to visiting scholars; should promote both national and international faculty exchange programs. And policies governing these faculty development efforts should not be so restrictive as to violate the spirit of the American Association of University Professors' understanding and wise views expressed in its document, "Statement of Principles on Leaves of Absence," which states in part the following: "All evidence that the leave will increase individual effectiveness or produce academically or socially useful results should be considered in evaluating applications. A leave may either involve specialized scholarly activity or be designed to provide broad cultural experience and enlarged perspective."

When Mimi Sheraton, who had been the *New York Times* restaurant critic for 7 years, resigned a few years back, she wrote that she wanted to stop eating for a while—thereby reminding all of us that burn-out need not be limited to challenging activities. Indeed, though the term "burn-out" may figure prominently in today's psychobabble, the condition to which it refers has been lamented by poets and dramatists from ancient Greece to modern America. Colors fade, sensations dim, interests weaken, enthusiasms diminish, and we find ourselves covering ever longer distances in first gear.

St. Augustine may have been right: We cannot define time. But we do know what it does, for we have all, to a greater or lesser degree, experienced its often devastating effects. To remain fully alive to all the colors of your world for a professional lifetime of teaching is no foothill to climb. A wise and caring administrator provides ropes and grapples and cleats. He might otherwise find himself with a kind of faculty whom W. H. Auden may have had in mind when referring to those who talk in someone else's sleep.

Though ordinarily one does not fault Dante for not placing nay-sayers in a circle beneath that occupied by mass murderers in the *Inferno,* any faculty member mourning over the corpse of an idea garroted by one in authority who habitually says "No"

may find it within himself to question the Italian poet's judgment. An academic administrator might profitably begin each day by reciting "Yes" in several languages. For those who wield power effectively for the greatest good of a university will not only persuade others to enter enthusiastically into their own dreams but will with equal vigor work to help others, particularly the faculty, to define and to realize their own. Understandably, one clings with a certain tenderness to one's own ideas and watches their development and implementation with an attentiveness and devotion rarely bestowed on the ideas of others. If an administrator therefore harnesses this source of ego-energy, everybody wins. The institution is alive with projects; the faculty are encouraged to invest time and energy in proposals that will be given serious and open consideration; and administrators bask in a climate that is conducive to intellectual growth.

While history records instances of personal intellectual growth under conditions of fear and insecurity, these instances are memorable precisely because they are exceptional. The mind works best when unencumbered by worries and unfettered by anxieties. Now while a college/university cannot eliminate from its faculty's lives the stresses and tensions of the human condition, it can and has supported its faculty's professional development by guaranteeing its intellectual freedom and thereby eradicating the universal fears associated with holding minority positions and defending unpopular conclusions.

The modish attack on tenure is being waged with all the decorum of the genteel: Under the pressure of declining enrollment and mounting inflation, is it not reasonable and fiscally responsible for dispassionate persons to reexamine a system that limits an institution's flexibility in responding quickly to appropriate shifts in demands for programs? However, while it may be reasonable to reexamine the practice of tenure, the tone of such questions, now posed on many campuses and at national meetings where administrators and faculty gather, clearly suggests that one should reexamine in order to abolish or to modify. The asking of questions has always been academe's favorite style of persuasion.

While large corporations boast of not having fired an employee for *x* number of years and while they make frequent use of the humane practice of "kicking professionals upstairs," university regents and boards of trustees in Colorado and elsewhere are dismantling the tenure system and several thus engaged are unable to disguise with pious phrases their barely contained glee at projecting a tough and business-like image. However, what is most demoralizing is not that lay persons, often appointed to governing boards in return for civic contributions that in no way qualify them to understand the culture of universities, should bear a grudge against a tenure system that has always been popularly interpreted simply as a perquisite, but that highly placed administrators should either remain silent or mistake the wreckers for repairmen. It is as if the wrecking ball were being viewed as the proper tool for serious renovation.

When newspapers now head columns with "Tenure Sparks Debate Among Higher Education Officials," you may feel fairly confident that what took place could be described as a debate only by those who would describe Thomas Aquinas's proofs for the existence of God as answers to a question. There was no question of the reality of God in the *Summa* and there are few debates about the absolute need for tenure among administrators in the foyers of the Hiltons. One after the mistaken other decision maker in academe bemoans the possible need to sacrifice tenure for a greater good. And when one raises a powerful voice to attack what is often referred to as the "sacred cow of academe" by suggesting that tenure be limited to 10 years with options to renew in 5-year increments, few stand to protest. Indeed, in the January 31, 1983, issue of *Newsweek*, an academic dean at a highly respected large midwestern university was quoted as saying, "I still believe in it [tenure], but from the point of view of an administrator, tenure is inconvenient." Honesty and tolerance—not to mention children and lovers—are all at times "inconvenient." One can only hope that the heady experience of being interviewed by a national weekly precipitated a temporary dizziness that accounts for the unfortunate choice of words.

Economically uncertain times have never been hospitable to minority views however carefully researched or seriously thoughtful and in the 1980s we have already seen signs of an ever-increasing desire to create a society of like-minded individuals. Witness the introduction of legislation to require school districts to teach creationism; the economic boycott of companies sponsoring certain television shows; the well-documented rise in school-board censorship of books—especially novels; conservative "Truth Squads" made up of citizens who enroll in courses to monitor the "truth" in statements made by professors; the specious yet influential arguments of some contemporary psychologists who claim that all who reach the highest level of morality will arrive at the same conclusions when addressing every moral dilemma.

Poll takers and social analysts are now claiming that idealism tempered by economics will characterize the spirit of the 1980s and the 1990s. We may well be into the decades of compromise when insisting upon the preservation of such worthy institutions as tenure in spite of "inconveniences" will be frowned upon as bad form. Academe played this scene of uncritical commitment to popular fancy in the 1960s, and is now spending much of its time and effort attempting to remedy the harm done by its capitulation, particularly with regard to academic standards. One can only hope that it will not step into this newly discovered stream without judging the nature of its current. If we are robbed, it may well be an inside job.

The intellectual vitality of a college/university is to a very significant degree determined by the intellectual vitality of its faculty. It follows, therefore, that academic administrators making decisions that touch upon the intellectual development and general welfare of its faculty should be guided by a spirit that demonstrates in every possible instance an unequivocal and celebrative belief in that truth. To be guided differently is to tempt faculty into intellectual apathy, a condition that is parasitic and ultimately spiritually life threatening. Compromise, or to use a more acceptable term, "moderation," will not do.

In medio stat virtus is a Roman adage that classics teachers have been fond of repeating. And at 15 or 16, when first introduced to it, few are prepared to argue that the Aristotelian concept, proclaiming that virtue is, indeed, to be found between extremes, is anything but good and true and beautiful. But however favorably disposed one may have been toward this high-sounding phrase, its use as a reliable guide for action may have appeared even then as more attractive than practical. If one visualized moderation as a point on a scale—not necessarily the absolute midway point—one was left with a variable sliding scale, for as the imagined extremes became more and more excessive, what had once blazed as madness could easily take on the glow of reasonableness.

Only many books later did one come to understand that this Western ideal of moderation was intimately connected with one of the games people play, namely, the manipulation of others. One of the more effective techniques used in this game is known to everyone: You ask for more than you really want so as to appear reasonable when you compromise and accept less. Anyone with a clever 6 year old who asks to be read four chapters of a book before going to bed in order to score points by settling for two suspects that man may be born with the rules programmed into some portion of the brain.

The manipulation of others is, of course, a game that is as old as man, and history is replete with accounts of very sophisticated moves. Our century, however, may be distinguished for having raised its "variable scale" technique to an art form, for we have actually created a profession dedicated (though not limited) to the pursuit of its perfection: advertising. We are conditioned to wear two rings and two bracelets by the model in *Harper's Bazaar* who wears 10 rings and a dozen bracelets as she lounges on pillows in the pasha's anteroom. We raise or lower skirts "in moderation" in direct proportion to the "excessively" long or short ones created by an Anne Klein, and we buy a "moderately" priced $9,000 car after we have test-driven the top of the line's $15,000 one. We are, after all, "reasonable" people.

When it comes to the width of ties and lapels, one might with amusement agree with Prufrock: "I am no prophet—and here's no great matter" and let those who wish wear the bottom of their trousers rolled. However, when the same technique of the game is applied to persuade—and even to manipulate—those who formulate policies in education, we are on a different plane of seriousness. To perceive beauty in clothes due to methods formulated by Dior is one thing; to perceive "reasonableness" in education due to methods formulated by Madison Avenue is another.

It is highly probable that in the past tumultuous 20 years in American colleges/universities, administrators set their imprimatur on certain educational policies out of a well-intended endorsement of moderation. Furthermore, it is equally probable that the moderate positions themselves were never closely scrutinized before being accepted because attention had been diverted to the extreme demands. Examples abound in such areas as criteria for admission, standards tolerated in remedial courses, levels of discourse accepted in college credit-bearing courses, truces signed in the development of curricula. Decisions made in these areas as in many others have at times most likely been formulated not out of conviction but out of appeasement. In truth, the decades of the 1960s and 1970s promoted their own brand of compromise, though social scientists accuse the 1980s of cultivating a safe personality.

Admittedly, the pressure to wear "moderate" opinions as

amulets to ward off diabolical "extremes" has not lost any no-
ticeable power and is now being applied to many issues such as
the appropriate assessment of students and the traditional rights
of faculty. Hence, it becomes imperative for administrators to take
the long view and to be strengthened by recalling the contributions
to this nation made by former academic decision makers whose
habits of the heart and convictions of the intellect led them to
plant trees that would in time provide shade for others.

Every academic administrator's decisions follow a route
mapped by the force of convictions, which, while periodically
tested and occasionally fine-tuned, should remain strong. The
courses of action suggested in the cases that follow are the result
of an unshakeable faith in the care an administrator should take
to cultivate a life of the mind, to focus energies on works that in
substance and style are in keeping with a college/university's distinctive mission, and to remember at all times the central role of
the faculty in achieving institutional excellence. Any number of
other defensible convictions might trace more dramatic journeys;
any number of managerial dicta might radiate from other beliefs
viewed as providing the major thrust to decision making. But no
administrator is likely to exercise effective leadership without bas-
ing his decisions on a system of values that he defends persua-
sively and applies consistently. And while this system should
undergo periodic checkups, any alteration made to it should come
as a result of a genuine change of mind and not as a result of
inertia or of pressures that are not always fully understood.

In 1572, the Venetian painter Veronese had to appear before the
Holy Office in Venice to defend himself against the charge of blas-
phemy. The Church wanted to know why, in a painting of the
Last Supper, Veronese had included such profane matters as people scratching themselves, loitering, and even in one case, having
a nosebleed. Veronese replied, "I thought these things might
happen."

All of the things that follow I thought might happen.

CHAPTER TWO
LET'S STORM THE BASTILLE
A CASE OF DISTURBANCES AND DISSENT

All campus organized demonstrations and orchestrated disruptions have causes other and deeper than those that allegedly precipitate them. That is, like wars, they have remote and proximate causes, and an effective and wise handling of them depends in part on interpreting the last act in light of the preceding ones. Students who overturn the tables and burn the brochures of Xerox recruiters at the college job fair feel compassion for the victims of South African apartheid, but they also fear their own country's long and unresolved struggle with racism. Students who boycott the university's cafeterias in support of a striking housekeeping staff sympathize with workers living on the rim of poverty, but they carry in addition to pickets subliminal images of their own worn parents walking home from mills and factories, or of their own pampered parents sipping coolers by kidney-shaped pools. In a word, every student who picks up a placard denouncing some villain carries in his backpack a cultural and emotional baggage that has moved him to leave the comfort of his room and to join a group of like-minded for the sake of a common cause. And while it may not be possible to identify the motivating factors for such an act within the minds and hearts of each protester, it is not only possible but essential to have a thorough and, if possible, a sympathetic understanding of both the remote and proximate cultural causes of dissent and disruption at any given time.

For example, to dismiss animal rights activists as vegetarian crackpots whose minds have been weakened by eating sunflower seeds in the California sun is not a promising way to initiate a dialogue with those who brake for animals and who are now threatening to free all the rabbits caged in the university's biology building. While it is not true that all men of good will reach the same conclusions even after interminable meetings, it is equally false that administrators are exempt from maintaining open and well-furnished minds.

THE BACKGROUND

The town is small (population 11,000), Southern, and committed
to conservatism in all matters religious and political. The university
is private, of nearly equal size (Full Time Equivalent Students-
8,500), and well endowed. Though it had originally been founded
by a Protestant denominational group, it has long since severed
all ties with the church but those that bind through courtesy. The
vast majority of students are undergraduates, though the institution does offer nine small but solid doctoral programs. Admission officers and department chairs have attracted students and
faculty primarily from within the state and from an area bounded
by five neighboring states. The campus by and large is cohesive,
the Floral Arrangement Society invites the president to its spring
tea, the local merchants dismiss the Greeks' infrequent and un-
creative Bacchanalias with nostalgic amusement.

Only one division within the university has bartered this subdued and peaceful atmosphere for one far more invigorating and
intense. The psychologists and biologists direct an Institute of
Animal Behavior that, while perhaps not distinguished, has for
some time been nationally, even internationally, known as the
source of excellent work. It had been founded 30 years ago by a
European-born woman who had studied under Konrad Lorenz
and published studies of great repute. Major research universities
had been unable to catch her however widely they had cast their
nets, for she had married a wealthy Southern gentleman farmer
who when asked if he had ever traveled much would look perplexed and reply, "Where would I have gone? I was born here."
To the university's great benefit, however, he considered it manly
to indulge his wife's eccentric interests. As a consequence, the
institute's building and laboratories are the envy of those who are
well traveled, and faculty research is often generously supported
by his private foundation.

The founding lady is now of a certain age and the flesh is
less willing than the spirit. However, the volume and quality of
the institute's work is impressive and widely recognized; its undergraduates are accepted in the most prestigious graduate
schools; its doctoral graduates are teaching across the country. As
a result, the profile of the carefully screened faculty and students
recruited by and attracted to the institute is considerably less provincial than that of the university as a whole. This difference has

been the source of a general minor tension and an occasional major dispute.

The psychologists and biologists and their students give signs of considering everyone on campus not associated with the institute to be comatose. Not to be outdone, the historians and sociologists have been heard to refer to the trees bordering the institute's building as "Palo Altos" and to the building itself as the "Harvard Coop."

THE HAPPENING

The institute's faculty, working singly or in small teams, have focused a significant portion of their research on the physiological regulation of emotion, and many of their experiments relate to the study of aggression and fear in cats, baboons, and rats.

MARCH 15

The cherry trees are in bloom; undergraduate applications for next year are 6% above projections; you have had a paper accepted by an editor who heretofore had found the strength to resist the charms of your prose; and all communications on your computer screen are nonlethal. Even the last message cannot break your "earth is the right place to be" mood. The director of student affairs simply wishes to alert you to noises coming from a small (40 or so members) fundamentalist Christian group that has sponsored a series of lectures this past month centering on the theme, "Abuse of the Helpless." The titles of the talks have suggested horror chambers: "The Aborted Child Screams," "Science's Cruelty to Animals," "Molestation of Children." The speakers have disappointed no one attracted by the titles. In the director of student affair's judgment, the tone of the meetings have become increasingly militant. He does not think that the group is about to turn its plowshares into swords, but it is exhibiting a mild hysteria that troubles him. A young assistant professor in his second year in the philosophy department has named himself the group's adviser. He has a lean and hungry look.

You have been receiving similar messages from Director S. for the 3 years you have been in office. In your salad days, before you knew that extreme right groups were his bête noire, you fingered these memos instead of worry beads as you fell asleep at night. But now you smile and take comfort in the familiar.

MARCH 19
You receive the following letter.

Dear Dr. _____:

We demand to know why you as chief academic officer and presumably a Christian are allowing the following to take place in the labs of the Institute of Animal Behavior on our campus.

While you read this, certain so-called scientists supported by our tuition payments are:

1. Depriving animals of food and drink and, then, provoking them to anger and fear
2. Surgically removing parts of the brain of animals, and, then, using stimuli to provoke rage
3. Using electrical shocks to certain parts of the brain to elicit attacks
4. Applying electricity to other parts of the body to provoke anger and fear

How would you like to have these things done to you? People have seen animals writhing in pain and others have heard their screams.

You have an obligation to protect God's innocent creatures from men who think that it's all right to sin if you're wearing a white lab coat while you do it.

This is what comes of hiring atheists for professors. We are not certain that there's a true Christian in either the psychology or the biology department.

Sincerely,

Christian Students For The
Protection of Animals (CSPA)
G. M., President
S. N., Secretary

MARCH 24

You spend an hour with G. M., a male in his third year, majoring in philosophy, and with S. N., a female in her second year, majoring in occupational therapy. They seem to have no evidence whatsoever that would support accusations that the institute's scientists are in violation of U.S. Public Health Department guidelines governing experiments conducted on animals, but the fires of their zeal are not dampened by a paucity of facts. Their rhetoric is that of the pulpit; their energy that of the crusader. They view rational discourse as a method favored by unbelievers and it becomes clear that they suspect you of being among them.

You assure them that you take the matter seriously and that you will investigate. They lower their visors, unsheath their swords and tell you that what they demand is an end to all experimenting on animals in the institute or elsewhere in the university and that 60 of them are prepared to sacrifice much to that end. Dr. P. of the philosophy department, their adviser, has convinced them that experiments can be simulated on computers. Consequently, the agony inflicted on animals is absolutely unnecessary and sadistic.

MARCH 25—A.M.

You speak to the head of the institute, who has been receiving abusive telephone calls and letters from CSPA members accusing him of running an animal concentration camp.

Is he in compliance with NIH guidelines for the humane care and use of laboratory animals?

Certainly, he is. His faculty have millions of dollars of grants and contracts.

Have the laboratories been inspected by any government agency recently? Say, in the past 6 months?

No, but he is certain that everything is in order. He knows and trusts his faculty.

He, of course, on a regular basis inspects the laboratories himself?

Oh, sure. Actually, he has been terribly busy meeting a deadline on a book in the past few months. But the final draft of the manuscript is now on his editor's desk and he will personally check almost immediately to see that all experiments are beyond reproach. He will get back to you soon. Meanwhile you should relax. At City they would throw these ignoramuses in the Hudson and watch them swim to Jersey. You really should not let yourself be intimidated by a handful of students who sport bumper stickers reading, "Beam me up, Jesus."

"Nor by a very bright, influential, tough faculty member" is the thought that reproaches you as you hang up rather too meekly for your subsequent comfort.

The bloom is off the cherry trees.

MARCH 25—P.M.

You confirm in writing the understanding you reached by telephone with the head of the institute and you set a deadline for his response. You want to be guaranteed within 2 weeks that all of the CSPA's concerns have been addressed and that the institute's research methodologies are in full compliance with the National Institute of Health's latest guidelines.

You write G. M. and S. N. and promise them a response within a month. Since their accusations are totally unsubstantiated, you conclude that while you have no cause to conduct a full-scale investigation, you do owe them the courtesy of reassuring them that the university would not take lightly cruelty of any kind and for any cause.

MARCH 26

The CSPA, positioned on every campus walkway, distributes handouts urging everyone to attend a rally the following day at noon in the quad facing the Institute of Animal Behavior. There all will be informed concerning what is taking place inside that building while insensitive non-Christian administrators compute tuition fees. Do you want to continue to support the cruelty of implanting electrodes in the brains of defenseless creatures? If not, attend the rally.

MARCH 27

Approximately 250 persons are assembled in front of the institute at noon: all 40 to 60 of the true believers, passers-by who would enjoy a happening at any Trafalgar Square, and two dozen students from the institute who are more amused than threatened and who take pleasure in hurling witticisms across the speakers' makeshift platform. All in all, a sort of baby Berkeley incident.

APRIL 2

As if enraged by the coolness of the administration's response to its accusations and the apparent apathy of a campus distracted by matters that it considers trivial by comparison to its cause, the mood of the CSPA turns ugly. Graffiti of the most offensive anti-Semitic kind are spray-painted on wall after wall of the institute during the night: "Jews Run Animal Buchenwald," "Jew-Scientist Go Back to New York," "Boston Kikes Go Home," "Free the University of Stanford Jews." By morning, the institute's main entrance has been chain locked and 40 or so members of the CSPA are lying on cardboard crosses in front of it hoping to be made worthy of martyrdom.

SUGGESTED COURSE OF ACTION

As a consequence of the conflagrations set by campus riots in the late 1960s, nearly all colleges/universities have installed smoke detectors and effective sprinkler systems that are known to everyone in authority and inspected annually. Hence, in this case the university will undoubtedly abide by a regulatory code specifying what manner of demonstrating is in keeping with an institution that supports free inquiry and what sanctions will be imposed for actions that violate such a code.

In all major policies and procedures, this code will most probably follow the principles outlined in the 1971 Carnegie Commission Report entitled, *Dissent and Disruption*. Hence, in a spirit of respect for and goodwill toward all individuals holding contrary views and in an effort to avoid precipitating violence, the director of student affairs will attempt to negotiate with the protesters. Presumably, there are other ways of entering and leaving the building whose main entrance is now being blocked, so the demonstration, while distracting, inconvenient, potentially dangerous, and in execrable taste, is interrupting neither instruction nor research. Given that, the university can afford to spend a reasonable amount of time negotiating and waiting for time and perhaps the discomfort of a heavy rainstorm to dissipate the crucified. The director of student affairs will take care to avoid humiliating the protesters and will shun ultimatums. To remind these students and their sympathizers, the numbers of which are unknown, that when all is said and done they are without real power is not a means of weakening their resolve. Furthermore, they do not deserve to have their tragedy reviewed as a comedy however jejune their drama.

If negotiation, repeated requests to leave the premises, and time prove weaker than the protesters' determination, the university may be obliged to use injunctions and even to forcibly remove the demonstrators. It cannot allow the main entrance to a campus building to be chain locked indefinitely; it cannot allow open defiance of its policies once negotiation has failed; it cannot allow the safety of the protesters to be threatened by nonsympathizers who may view the university as having been stared down. Once the incident is over, disciplinary action or legal action may follow depending on what codes and laws have been broken.

Most probably, the director of student affairs will have enacted or coordinated most of the university's responses to the actual acts of rebellion: the defacing of the building with graffiti and the blocking of the main entrance to the institute. However, you bear very direct responsibility for addressing the problem of the exposed lacunae in the minds of possibly 60 students and an unknown number of closet sympathizers.

It is all well and good to refuse to adopt barbaric methods to quell barbaric acts, but a defense of free expression does not preclude convictions. Hatred is not to be preferred to love; bigotry and tolerance are not of equal worth; ignorance is not due the same respect as knowledge; and miniterrorism is s still terrorism. What began perhaps as a sincere concern for the alleged infliction of unnecessary suffering on animals, ended in a very disturbing display of bigotry and antiintellectualism.

Your challenge here, as is often the case elsewhere, is not to apply the proper management technique, but to exercise the appropriate and expected leadership. Those who spray-painted the walls of the institute and those who lay on crosses before its door constituted no ordinary crowd, but a crowd made up of your students. However, like all other crowds, its inner life's most striking trait, especially after it has been dispersed, will be a feeling of persecution. As the social psychologist Elias Canetti made clear in his massive study, *Crowds and Power*, once a crowd has nominated its enemies, "These can behave in any manner, harsh or conciliatory, cold or sympathetic, severe or mild—whatever they do will be interpreted as springing from an unshakable malevolence, a premeditated intention to destroy the crowd, openly or by stealth" (*Crowds and Power*, The Seabury Press, New York, 1978, p. 22). Hence, you should expect that your attempts to encourage the demonstrators and their sympathizers to examine without prejudice their premises and to engage in open and sincere dialogue with members of the academic community whose convictions differ from their own will be made most difficult by your having been labeled an enemy. But moguls are always there to be taken.

With the advice and consent of the executive committee of the university senate, or its equivalent, establish an ad hoc committee of faculty and students (including members of the institute) to consider the best ways and means of addressing what this episode has revealed. It seems highly probable that in this instance even if the proximate cause of the protest, alleged cruelty to animals, were eliminated by ordering an end to the use of animals in scientific experiments, the remote causes would remain and might even gain strength by feeding on a victory. All of your students, even those whose minds and hearts hide behind steel grates, should be given the opportunity to study the emotional and cultural underpinnings upon which they have built their world view.

Offering workshops, lectures, seminars, special topic courses, and debates that focus on themes related to the remote causes of the protest should benefit all but those so shameless as to boycott them. Some subjects central to this discourse come immediately to mind: the meaning of civil disobedience, appropriate forms of dissent in a free society, the nature and consequences of bigotry, and, of course, the use of animals in research. However, others perhaps less obvious are of equal importance. For example, the long-standing dispute in America between science and religion and the numerous attempts at reconciliation that have often satisfied neither scientists nor theologians is certainly relevant. As is the image in American culture of the scientist who continues to be ridiculed as someone who though well meaning is a bumbling, physically awkward person who has trouble keeping his rimless glasses from slipping off his nose, and who is considerably less at home in the universe than the animals he studies—witness the award-winning film *Never Cry Wolf*. And when American scientists in novels and drama and films and television are not falling through the ice, or tripping over their equipment, or setting their laboratories on fire, they turn mean and hide behind a mathematics no layman can understand so as to work secretly on experiments that threaten us all. What fears do these images mask?

While your ad hoc committee is coordinating a study of these topics and possibly of others, the chair of the philosophy department should not only encourage his young colleague who had appointed himself as adviser to the CSPA to take part in all of the efforts to provide insight into a serious event on campus, but should make certain that he understands the injustice of billing students for one's own romantic self-indulgence. In Italo Calvino's *Baron in the Trees*, the father tells his defiant son, Cosimo: "Rebellion cannot be measured by yards. Even when a journey seems no distance at all, it can have no return."

Now, while attending to remote causes is nearly always more intellectually exciting than attending to proximate ones, obviously you cannot walk to the library and forget the latter. Hence, you should make certain that:

1. The Institute of Animal Behavior's experiments are in strict compliance with the latest National Institute of Health guidelines and with those established by the American Psychological Association. The head of the institute should write you, say every 6 months or every year, guaranteeing that such is the case.
2. The institute's faculty consider using alternatives, such as computer simulation, to animals in research and be prepared to defend its decisions.
3. Since experiments on animals have important implications for our understanding of human behavior, no research in the institute is interrupted and no changes are made as a result of intimidation.

Note the impressive acceleration of the CSPA's moves and remember that a crowd of true believers is always afraid to lose its members through inaction. While you cannot afford to act precipitously, protesters can, for they seek drama while you want to avoid it.

Somewhere, sometime, a crowd will not want to brake for you. It is wise to have planned when to stand firm and when to jump high.

CHAPTER THREE
SHE ASKED FOR IT
A CASE OF SEXUAL HARASSMENT

That the title of this case does not refer to a request for the beautification of the campus will come as no surprise to anyone who has sat on either side of a desk in a college/university campus. The sentence has become the idiom of choice in the ritual defense of faculty accused of serious sexual harassment.

A measure both of the fairly recent attention focused on "harassment" as an abuse of power and of the equally recent concern that the spill of this offense may darken the lives of our students is made evident by all of us who lay stress now on the first syllable of the word now on the second.

Most colleges/universities know or suspect that this enemy to fairness and justice has scaled their walls, but few have reached a consensus as to its size and its strength, and virtually none is dispassionate when deciding on defensive strategies. Those institutions that have conducted studies and have shared data, such as Arizona State, Iowa State, Berkeley, Michigan State, and the University of Florida among others, have all come to essentially the same conclusion: between 20 and 30% of the women students on American campuses have been sexually harassed by male faculty. Another much smaller percentage of all students have had to deal with homosexual advances.

In *The Lecherous Professor* (Beacon Press, Boston, 1984), a study of sexual harassment on campus, Dzeich and Weiner point out that according to the National Center for Educational Statistics 6,374,005 women were enrolled in American colleges and universities in 1982, and that "If only 1 percent of all college women experienced sexual harassment, there would be 63,740 women victims." The very citing of these numbers frames a small and quivering symbol of the pathos associated with this topic. As if, unmoved by ideals of justice and by frequent empirical evidence that such ideals are not cherished, academicians had to be persuaded by data to offer all of their students the protection of the university and the full opportunities of the university's way of life.

THE BACKGROUND

Your midsize (FTES 14,500), public, urban midwestern university is known regionally for its success in the fine arts. The theater arts department is especially alive and attractive to increasingly sophisticated and talented students. Its productions are intellectually demanding and provide a grateful community more substantial fare than that offered at dinner theaters. The faculty are creative and encourage border crossings into neighboring states: music and dance. Their artistic disdain for bureaucratic rules is well within bounds, and they respect you when they cannot ignore you, for they have heard of administrators who have never read Ibsen and never seen a Pinter. Indeed, the only problem not associated with promotion, tenure, budget, or curriculum in the past 3 years concerned a male freshman who, under the influence of a book on New York art happenings in the 1950s, had climbed a tree near the university's theater and sat naked in one of its lower branches until a passing motorist had veered off the road. All agreed that you had handled the incident in a calm and judicious manner.

THE HAPPENING

MARCH 10—9:30 A.M.

SECRETARY: There's a father of one of our students on the phone and he insists on speaking to the person in charge of faculty. He won't tell me what it's about, but it's clear that he's very upset.

YOU: I'll take the call. Good morning. This is Mr. Y. speaking. May I help you.

FATHER: My name is Bob Clark and my daughter, Pamela, is a junior at the university. I'm calling to find out what kind of a dirty atheist slum you're running.

YOU: Listen, Mr. Clark . . .

FATHER: No, I won't listen. You're the one who's going to listen. We're decent churchgoing people my wife and me and she smashed her leg 2 years ago so I've had to go back to work at the canning factory on the night shift and I'm not so well myself and now we have to take all of this.

YOU: What is it that you have to take, Mr. Clark? I want to help you, but you must tell me precisely what the problem is that led you to call me.

FATHER: I'll tell you exactly what the problem is. Pamela was attacked right on your campus by a professor old enough to be her father and I want that man fired. For months my wife and me we wondered what was wrong with Pamela. She wouldn't hardly talk to us. Just sit in her room and play records. Her report card wasn't good and she'd go whole days without eating. Well, last night she broke down sobbing and told us what was wrong. I thank God her brother doesn't know because he'd go up to your fancy offices and kill somebody and no decent person would blame him. Now you fire this Dr. L. or I'm going to get me a lawyer. I want to know. Are you going to fire him, yes or no?

YOU: Mr. Clark, this is a very grave matter and I need more information before I make a decision.

FATHER: Yeah, victims don't have any rights in this country anymore. You for criminals walking the streets?

YOU: Mr. Clark, listen. I'm very much concerned about Pamela and about you also. I will begin an immediate investigation of these charges. What I would like to do is to meet with Pamela as soon as possible. If she's at home now, could I speak to her to arrange for a meeting?

MARCH 10—3:30 P.M.

PAMELA: I find it hard to talk about this, so I wrote it down for you.

To Whom It May Concern:

Last year at this time I was taking a course called, "Scenery Design II" taught by Ms. Coller. In order to get experience in scene designing, I volunteered to help on the sets for a production of "Cabaret" which the Musical Theater majors were preparing as their spring show. Dr. L. was directing the scenery design work and was the cause of the most traumatic experience of my life.

The act of violation against me took place six months ago last week. One night after the others had left, Dr. L. and I sat around talking in the mainstage area of the Theater Arts building. Without warning he started kissing me and petting me. It was dark and I stumbled about. I was scared to death because I knew it wasn't right, but I wasn't about to make him angry. Besides, I couldn't believe that this was happening. I mean that a professor that we all admired was doing this. It was surreal and I was so confused and shocked that for a minute I thought I was having a nightmare. I finally realized that my only hope was to push him away and to run out.

I quit the show but ever since then I have felt threatened by this man. The only person I told about this when it happened was my best friend who is also majoring in Theater Arts. She told me not to do anything, to just forget it happened because he could ruin my career here at the university.

I've been nervous and depressed ever since.

Sincerely,

Pamela Clark

YOU: Pamela, why did you wait 6 months before reporting this?

PAMELA: I didn't know where to go to report it. I didn't think that anyone would believe something that gross was done by a man who's so well liked. I was scared. I mean my best friend may have been right: Dr. L. has a lot of friends in the department and I have to take their courses.

YOU: Why are you telling me this now?

PAMELA: I've felt alone for months so I joined the Women's Center. I went to a workshop there last week where they explained what to do about things like this and they told us we owed it to others to speak up. After the workshop, I spoke to the director of the Women's Center and she gave me a lot of support. I told my mother and father too, but I shouldn't have. They're hysterical.

YOU: How well had you known Dr. L. before this incident took place? Had you spoken to him about matters unrelated to your work on the sets? And why was the main stage area dark?

PAMELA: We had put out the lights because everyone else had left and we were about to leave also. We were just sitting on the edge of the stage. I often talked to him a lot about all kinds of things. For example, I had broken up with my boyfriend at the beginning of that spring semester and we talked about that. A few times late at night I'd wait around and just chat with him. I mean I liked him, and all the women on campus think that he's good looking. But I didn't do anything wrong if that's what you're asking. He's a sick man.

YOU: Were there incidents on any of these occasions that made you uncomfortable?

PAMELA: No. I trusted him. I mean he's a middle-aged man and professors are supposed to help you. I never even imagined that anything like this could happen.

YOU: This incident took place months ago. How has Dr. L. behaved toward you since then?

PAMELA: I'm not in his classes and I don't work on shows he works on so I rarely see him. When I bump into him in the halls he doesn't even look at me. It's like I don't exist and it never happened.

YOU: Do you wish to tell me anything else?

PAMELA: Well, Dr. L. will probably tell you so I might as well. But it doesn't excuse him. I called him at home once or twice. He's separated from his wife and lives alone. He had told me he was lonely. And once when he asked me to go to the cafeteria for coffee I did. And maybe I flirted a little with him that once. But I didn't mean anything by it. I was just thanking him for having been nice to me and listening to me.

YOU: Pamela, you understand the seriousness of these charges?

PAMELA: Yes. He deserves whatever he gets. I didn't do anything wrong.

YOU: Do you want to change anything? Add anything?

PAMELA: No. I want that man off campus before he does this kind of thing again. And he will.

MARCH 15—11:00 A.M.

YOU: You got my letter outlining the charges?

DR. L.: Yes. It was a letter which I had been expecting for a long
time. It's almost a relief to have finally received it.

YOU: Did the incident take place?

DR. L.: Yes, it did. I wish I could deny it and remain truthful, but
I can't.

YOU: Did it happen the way the student claims it did?

DR. L.: Essentially, yes. She had been pursuing me for a couple
of months. She'd hang around at night and want to talk
after the other students had left; she'd be waiting for me
after classes; she haunted my office; she'd call me at home
two and three times a week and ask to come over.

YOU: Did she?

DR. L.: No. I was flattered by the attention and attracted to her,
but I knew that she was dazzled by what she took for sophistication. My wife had left me and I was lonely. At 48
it's nice to still feel wanted. She would leave notes in my
textbooks and pin others on my office bulletin board. But
look, I have no excuse, only a few feeble, cliché explanations right out of *Psychology Today*. I'd give anything to
relive the night to which she refers. I'm so ashamed I don't
even look at her and say Hello when we pass on campus.
I'm also worried about the effect of all this on her. Please
believe that I had never done anything like this before.
I've been here 12 years and I've given my all to this university.

YOU: I know you have.

DR. L.: I'm worried sick, so let me be blunt. Will this cost me my
job?

YOU: It's already cost you a great deal. But I don't know yet
what the total cost will be. I need time to think this
through, but I promise to reach a conclusion as soon as I
can. You know that I would not add to a sanction the anxiety of a delayed decision.

DR. L.: Thanks. I want you to know that I've spoken to Tom (the
chair of the theater arts department). He said that he had
asked to see you about this.

YOU: Yes. He's coming this afternoon at 2:30 p.m.

MARCH 17—2:30 P.M.

CHAIR: Look, Dr. L. is one of the three who are absolutely indispensable to the success of the department. The fellow's creative and totally dedicated. Counselors from all over the state send kids here because of him.

YOU: The charge is serious and he admits guilt. We don't even need an investigation to find out if what the student claims is true.

CHAIR: All right, but damn it you can't ruin a man's life because he made a pass at a woman. He shouldn't have done it, but he's going through a tough passage right now and this student bombshell is no innocent. Believe me. She'd been asking for this for months. The guy couldn't walk from his office to his class but that she spanieled at his heels—to coin a phrase. The department is ready to fight for this man. Be sure of that.

YOU: What do you think should be done?

CHAIR: Write him a letter of reprimand and tell the student to stop running after faculty. Trust me. I know this man. He's learned a terrible lesson. I imagine that the hysterical women-libbers want him hanging on a gibbet in front of the library? Something like this will never happen again.

YOU: The director of the Women's Center is coming to see me the day after tomorrow.

MARCH 19—4:00 P.M.

DIRECTOR: We're not asking for something that a university should be unwilling to give. All we want is justice for a student who has been badly abused. Pamela sat in my office for 2 hours after the center's workshop on sexual harassment and wept and wept. She feels terribly guilty for having flirted with Dr. L., but on some level knows that it's not her fault. Surely, no one in this institution is primitive enough to believe that a just punishment for flirting is sexual assault.

YOU: What do you think should be done?

DIRECTOR: Dr. L. should be dismissed as a tenured member of this faculty. He has abused both his power and the trust this community placed in him.

YOU: This university has never before dismissed a tenured faculty member. You realize that board regulations would call for a full public hearing if we were to impose that sanction.

DIRECTOR: Good. It's a perfect opportunity to teach this campus a lesson. We should let the entire community know what we stand for.

SUGGESTED COURSE OF ACTION

Place the professor on leave without pay for a period of one semester. A subsequent substantiated charge should trigger proceedings for permanent dismissal.

Both the accuser and the accused tell essentially the same story. The only difference in the telling of the tale is the degree of emphasis placed on the student's pursuit of the professor. Dr. L. sees himself as having been tempted beyond his strength, but understands that his demonstration of weakness is precisely what the institution finds objectionable. Pamela sees herself as having engaged in a mild flirtation, and does not believe that her behavior would have led to such consequences if Dr. L. had not been "sick." Both have most probably given you an accurate description of their view of the incident.

In Dr. L.'s defense, he has been with the university 12 years and no other charges have ever been brought against him; he is both truthful and contrite; the incident took place 6 months ago and he has not approached the student or made any attempt to speak to her since; the student did over a period of several months send out flirtatious if not amorous signals. However, in an institution dedicated to the preservation and cultivation of what is best in people, the "concern" in the "to whom it may concern" letter should ideally refer not only to one to whom the content pertains, but to one for whom the content matters. While Pamela may or may not be the naive maiden, a professor's abuse of power should not be measured by the innocence or experience of his victims. In weighing "She Asked for It" as against "He Should Have Known Better" standards of professional ethics tip the scale against Dr. L.

If you and Dr. L. reach accord on the appropriateness of the sanction that you have imposed, the matter between you is officially closed. Most campuses have by now detailed policies and procedures applying to cases of sexual harassment, but committees of peers normally sit for the purpose of determining guilt or innocence and not for the purpose of imposing sanctions. In this case, the guilt is not in question. However, the national AAUPs "Procedures For Imposition of Sanctions Other Than Dismissal" (AAUP *Policy Documents and Reports,* 1984, p. 27) states "If the administration believes that the conduct of a faculty member, although not constituting adequate cause for dismissal, is sufficiently grave to justify imposition of a severe sanction, such as suspension from service for a stated period, the administration may institute a proceeding to impose such a severe sanction . . ."

Two questions follow that only appear scholastical. One, in the use of the word "may" as in "may institute," is the AAUP giving an administrator permission to institute a hearing or is it giving an administrator an option to institute a hearing? Two, the AAUP does not define "severe" as opposed to "minor" sanction, though it chooses as an example of the first the very penalty recommended in this instance. Now, suspension from service for a year might well be a minor sanction for deliberately setting a fire that destroys a laboratory and a written reprimand that becomes part of a permanent record for leering at a member of the opposite sex might well be considered severe. In a word, there is no "minor" or "severe" out of context and "minor" and "severe" within context is always a judgment call. Of course if your local AAUP chapter has not met since World War II, you may (option not permission) decide to ignore text analysis.

At any rate, the spirit of all AAUP policies that pertain call for informal discussions between faculty members and appropriate administrative officers in order to look toward a mutual settlement. This same spirit should guide your actions in a case where the accused admits guilt and where a hearing could serve no purpose but to tack a description of the sins on the church door. Never make an example of anyone. If a professor's offense is so grave as to merit the ruination of his career, then, dismiss the professor; do not call for an *auto-de-fe.*

Write Dr. L. describing your sanction, your reasons for it, your expectations for the future. Copy the chair of the theater arts department.

Write the student informing her that action has been taken without specifying the nature of it. Offer the services of the Counseling Center.

Call Student Services and ask an appropriate staff member to offer to work with the student.

Write the father informing him that the university has conducted an investigation and is satisfied with the action it has taken. Do not describe this action or reveal any of the information given you by either the daughter or Dr. L. Should the father seek to pursue the matter through an attorney, direct all communications to the university's attorney.

Be certain that the university's attorney approves all of the preceding correspondence for legal sufficiency.

Hold a meeting with the director of the Women's Center for the purpose of exchanging views on the problem of sexual harassment in general and the spirit that should inform the combat against it on your campus in particular. Suggest that the center plan a series of lectures and panel discussions on the topic to which all members of the academic community would be invited. Give this effort financial as well as moral support.

To seek an equitable solution to a sexual harassment case in a culture where *Penthouse* and *Ms.* vie for attention at drugstores is to live life without a net. The convoluted language and outright silliness of some university documents on this question attest to the difficulty of remaining calm and wise when the very essence of an issue arouses passion in all but the dead. However, while myopia might be mistaken for ogling, discriminating on the basis of sex by word or deed is recognizable by all persons of goodwill. The task, no mean one, is to protect and to defend the rights of both our faculty and our students when those inspired by a passion to prosecute or to defend one or the other would enshrine causes and ignore people.

If you are ever tempted to teach the university a lesson, change your shoes and run around the administration building five times.

CHAPTER FOUR

THE THURSDAY CLUB
REVIEWS THE NUDES

A CASE OF ACADEMIC FREEDOM

When ivy still grew on college walls, disputes between campuses and the communities that contained them were often referred to as "town and gown" controversies. Now, in an era of glass and prestressed concrete, similar disagreements may be filed under headings far less poetic, such as "pending litigation" or "potential lawsuits." However, the two most active catalysts in activating a community's outrage against faculty and/or students are the same now as then: too little patriotism or too much sex. That is, what an often very vocal minority views as "too little" or "too much."

While more and more faculty in the past 30 years have doffed their medieval gowns and climbed down from the ivory tower to advise government officials, to share the results of their research with business and industry, to work toward social change; and while administrators have exchanged their tweed jackets with the leather elbow patches for navy pin-striped suits and often manage institutions of higher education as genuine CEOs would, the fact remains that "the ivory tower" is simultaneously an appropriate and effective myth and metaphor. A university is, by its very nature, an institution "set aside" for the purpose of preserving, sharing, and advancing knowledge. While it, as it should, reaches out to the world of commerce and the world of government, it can only fulfill its mission by maintaining enough distance to preserve both its freedom and its integrity.

As a result, most communities are proud and even grateful to have a university located within its borders, but they rarely become completely at ease with it. They always approach it *endimancher*, as the French say, somewhat self-consciously formal. This tension, as necessary and as healthy as it is, can at times become excessive and snap the ties that bind the university to a group within the community; then, of course, repairs must be made immediately, for a university needs the goodwill of its neighbors.

THE BACKGROUND

She dresses only in black, prefers boots to shoes, and long capes to coats in all seasons. She has attracted attention on campus, not only by her unusual dress, but by her mildly disruptive antiadministration attacks at Faculty Senate meetings. Last year, she was photographed by the local morning daily newspaper as she appeared before a state hearing commission studying the question of comparable worth. She called the members of the commission "eunuchs" and was escorted out of the state house by a marshal. She is a tenured assistant professor on your faculty, and a very fine artist. Colleagues respect her as a professional and tolerate her antics; students flock to her classes for two reasons. One, she is apparently a gifted and caring teacher, and, two, if the professor wears a cape, this must be art.

THE HAPPENING

The members of your art department, on a rotating basis, mount exhibits of their works, and this spring, this assistant professor's new series of pen-and-ink drawings are being shown in one of the campus's galleries. You attend the opening night reception with some eagerness, for you have admired her previous shows, which have displayed her watercolors, and you now look forward to seeing what she has done in a new medium. The drawings are striking and lovely; with the greatest economy of line, she has captured the grace of the human body. Fully one-half of the works displayed, possibly inspired by Picasso's late drawings, have as subject matter men and women experiencing sexual pleasure: both heterosexual and homosexual. Of the 150 or so who attend the reception, half are faculty and students from the College of Fine Arts and half are local and regional artists, curators, critics, and friends. The occasion is festive, the artist is jubilant, and the critics are impressed. Indeed, two say so in the next day's newspaper, and one in a late-night spot on radio. You are genuinely pleased by the event and by the faculty member's talent, so the next morning you start your day by writing her a note wherein you thank her and congratulate her, and, then, go on to other matters. The show has been scheduled to last from April 1 to June 1.

Two weeks later, the president of the Thursday Club, a social organization of women who occasionally raise funds for local cultural events, writes you a letter that makes opening your mail a dangerous act. Members of her organization, lured by the laudatory reviews of the campus's latest exhibit, had organized a tour of the show and had been both shocked and embarrassed by its content and ask for its immediate removal. Otherwise, the Thursday Club will have no choice but to write the chair of the university's Board of Visitors, who happens to be the club president's brother and a significant contributor to the alumni fund, to lodge a formal complaint and to withdraw forever its previous support of what was under the leadership of your predecessor a very fine and moral place. Furthermore, she and her friends in the club remember well having seen in the morning paper a picture of the faculty member (she will not deign to call her an artist) who drew these disgusting pictures being escorted out of the state house by a policeman. She had meant at that time to write and urge her dismissal, but she had concluded that you would have enough sense to do it without her urging. She sees now that she was wrong, and she is most disappointed in you and in the university. The president of the Thursday Club has copied the chair of the art department, who finds the letter amusing enough to share with a few members of his faculty. Within a day or two, one of these faculty members uses the letter in class to illustrate his perception of life as a struggle between the vulgar philistines and the liberating artists. Inspired by the professor's lecture and the season of spring, the "Students for the Liberation of Art" organize a promotional campaign for the show that rivals any that would have been put together by a vulgar bourgeois. Faculty, students, administrators, and members of the community, who had to ask for directions in order to reach the campus art gallery housing the exhibit, swell the attendance record far beyond the student–promoters' hope. Some faculty, who are by now enjoying themselves, are supporting an extended run, and everyone but everyone has an opinion about both the show and the action you should take. As you wish for a distracting freak spring blizzard, the letters that arrive are about evenly divided between those advocating freedom of expression and those deploring the unraveling moral fiber of academe.

SUGGESTED COURSE OF ACTION

Do not close the exhibit. The principle of academic freedom is worth any number of threats and any amount of abuse. Attending to this situation will take hours out of your administrative life, may force you to neglect temporarily other issues, and may even earn you the scorn and enmity of former benefactors. However, you could hardly be devoting time and energy to the defense of a more important philosophical concept than that of academic freedom. And you should be careful in a case such as this one not to allow the indiscretion of the department chair, the self-indulgence of the faculty lecturer, and the well-intended but complicating student activities to distract you from the central issue: the rights of the faculty artist, which you must protect.

While there is little doubt that the former political activities and nonconformist behavior and dress of the artist are probably influencing the responses of at least some who have taken part in this happening, there is no doubt that you must guard against allowing it to affect you. You have no evidence that your lady in black intended this show as a political act even though she is now having the time of her life and has not hidden her satisfaction at seeing you in a nonenviable position. In addition, the question of intent is not of the essence. Even if the artist had wanted, in-cidentally, to *épater le bourgeois,* the fact is that her colleagues, both in the university's art department and in the departments of other local colleges/universities, and local and regional art critics had all acknowledged her considerable talent and the beauty of her drawings. No one in the field had even referred to the propriety or impropriety of the subject matter.

Though the gallery does not close, though the drawings re-main firmly mounted to the wall, you do not extend the dates of the originally announced run. To do so would be unnecessarily provocative and certainly damage, if not ruin, your chances of restoring goodwill. And goodwill must be restored. To accept lethargically the permanent ill will of the side that lost as the price you necessarily had to pay for the defense of those whose views you supported would be a serious mistake. You should have all during the controversy and for some time after the events ex-plained your philosophical position and every aspect of your de-cision to anyone who would listen and even to those who made believe not to. These 3 or 4 very trying weeks are an excellent

.

time to teach certain aspects of the academic culture to members of the community and to members of a faculty and student body who have a right to know why you arrive at certain decisions. Lunch with the chair of the university's Board of Visitors, tea with the members of the Thursday Club, short but persuasive addresses to the university senate, the art department, the student government association, and an office coffee hour with the "Students for the Liberation of Art" are all possible forums for a candid discussion of the value of academic freedom and the ways in which one might unintentionally weaken it. You will not persuade everyone, but you will be judged by the way you have tried.

A university that does not defend academic freedom is no university at all.

CHAPTER FIVE
A HOUSE OF CARDS
A CASE OF DEPARTMENTAL MISMANAGEMENT

The poet Edith Sitwell, who was once described by the novelist Elizabeth Bowen as "a high altar on the move," said of herself, "I couldn't possibly wear tweeds. . . . People would follow me on bicycles." The remark is clever and amusing in part because Englishmen of a certain class in the Edwardian era and for some-time thereafter characteristically wore tweeds when they rode bicycles. I do not imagine that many traits other than the manner of dressing when riding a bicycle distinguished upper-class bicycle riders from nonbicycle riders in the British Isles in the early decades of the twentieth century. Thus man, never satisfied with an all-inclusive genus or even species, always itching to examine parts, found in this instance as in so many others yet another small way of inventing a subcategory. In our long history we have used an infinite number of headings to bring the world to heel. These range from race, age, nationality, creed, and language, to economic status to political affiliation, to taste in the arts, to the chosen length of haircuts, to the preference in the width of lapels. It is as if nothing spoke to man directly; as if any attempt to apprehend things whole were unmanageable, even threatening.

Consequently, within large organizations, the necessary creation of divisions and subdivisions based on purpose and function serve not only to distribute responsibility, but to satisfy in an admirable fashion this seemingly primitive need to differentiate. "What can one say? He's an artist." "You expect practicality? Come on, she's a philosopher." "Don't worry, she'll negotiate. She's a political scientist." "He's outgoing. After all, he's a salesman." Since these groupings, at times called teams or divisions, in business or industry are frequently oriented toward accomplishing very specific and self-contained tasks and toward pursuing short-term goals, the teams or divisions need not be permanent and are, indeed, more effective when formed or re-formed in endless permutations based upon the solving of a particular problem, say, the streamlining of communications between a central bank and its branch offices, or upon meeting a specific end, say, winning the national league pennant.

Colleges/universities as complex organizations have not escaped the need to divide the whole. The groupings are called "disciplines" in academia and "departments" on campuses. However, the academic discipline's goals are long term and not specific-task oriented. One cannot easily imagine the demise of research in chemistry or the end of the teaching of philosophy, and no one thinks of "getting this class of seniors out by the May 20 commencement deadline" or of "putting an end to this problem of Being." Furthermore, initiation into these groups is both long and arduous and dependent upon a shared passion. Hence, the academic groupings are by and large exceedingly stable. Fearing the strength of such stability, and, under the best circumstances, cohesiveness, and somewhat dissatisfied with the single-minded devotion to the domain of any one discipline, some colleges/universities in the late 1960s and early 1970s attempted to dismantle departments. To little avail. Experiments to group disciplines into configurations other than those of the traditional departments have been by and large unsuccessful and short-lived. What those impatient for reform failed to recognize was the role of the academic department as psychological nesting ground. What substitute could be as enticing as a guarantee that however high you soared and however far you migrated, you could return to birds of the same plumage? Managerial ease? Increased communication between fiefdoms? Surely you jest.

The Roman Petronius, who like all satirists may be suspected of a vitriolic disposition and a jaundiced eye, wrote some 2,000 years ago: "We trained hard . . . but it seemed every time we were beginning to form up into teams we would be reorganized. I was to learn later in life that we tend to meet any new situation by reorganizing; and a wonderful method it can be for creating the illusion of progress while producing confusion, inefficiency, and demoralization." The words may apply to many corporations where a 2-year-old flowchart is as dependable as last year's airline schedule of flights, but they do not apply to academic disciplines nor to most campus departments.

All groupings of persons, even that of an academic department, can and do take on many of the atavistic strengths and weaknesses of the tribe. When they work well, they nurture and initiate the young; they support the weak and encourage the strong; they rejoice in the success of its members and sympathize in their sorrow. Above all, they give those within a profession a home, with all of the familiarity and sense of belonging which that word connotes. But when they work badly, they encourage intellectual provincialism and civil discord. Those within seek an exit; those without avoid the entrance. And thereby hangs a tale.

THE BACKGROUND

Yours is a private college located in an urban New England setting. It had been founded at the turn of the century as a spark from the flint of Protestant zeal and had attracted a steady 200-odd freshmen a year until a post–World War II stampede had pushed enrollments up to a record 1,800 FTES. Since 1955 your programs have been in the arts and sciences, nursing, occupational therapy, health sciences, speech and hearing disorders, and communication arts. The institution is described by those indifferent to its success as steady, comfortable, friendly, well-intended, and sleepy. It has for the most part attracted and selected a laissez-faire, competent administration and faculty. The books are balanced, the social and cultural events are taken seriously, persons linger over coffee after lunch, and the students send professors Christmas cards. The faculty are devoted to the students, who return the affection, become loyal alumni, find jobs, pay their taxes, and vote.

A precipitous decline in enrollment in the liberal arts program and an only somewhat less worrisome one in nursing a few years back came as an unwelcome noise in the night that was loud enough to wake everybody. At 62, the president objected to being awakened in this rude manner, bought himself a fishing pole, and moved to the Rockies from whence he mails postcards that under the circumstances seem objectionably cheerful. The board of trustees chose as his successor a young CEO with neon, multicolored political ambitions whose solution to the significant enrollment drop had been to institute a business management major. Not conspicuously creative a solution, but the thing that matters about success is that it is not failure. Within 6 years some 600 FTE students were studying management techniques and registering for introductory courses in the humanities in order to meet general college requirements.

THE HAPPENING

The faculty awakening had begun in fear and ended in discontent. While grateful that the enrollment has stabilized, the tenured faculty find themselves vaguely disquieted and somewhat embarrassed by the size of their relieved anxiety. It is as if their treasured and polished image of themselves as idealists driving battered automobiles in order to buy books and subscriptions to the symphony had suddenly revealed a pentimento. As if, beneath a surface painting wiped thin by worries of not meeting the mortgage payments, they had discovered an attachment to lawn furniture and self-cleaning ovens. They found it difficult to feel affection for a president who had forced them none too gently to look into a mirror, and equally difficult to welcome a department filled with people who viewed themselves as having rescued the ineffectual and the unpopular.

True, the liberal arts faculty had for years worked, and worked amicably and sympathetically, with faculty of preprofessional programs (e.g., nursing, occupational therapy, etc.), but all such faculties had been service oriented, folded into an existing structure slowly and carefully, and, above all, been perceived as given to the pursuit of similar truths and dreams. They all wore with the same degree of grace the same shabby flannels, all dressed their homes in uncoordinated fabrics, all dreamed of sabbaticals in small villages in Normandy. Now in the dining room they sat across from colleagues who wore pin-striped suits and spoke offhandedly of their places at the Cape and their spring skiing in Chile. These aliens could not attend certain committee meetings because they were busy as consultants to local firms. Indeed, they were conspicuous in demonstrating little interest in the affairs of the college. Consequently, when word began to circulate that all was not well in the department of the rescue squad, not even self-preservation could prevent a slight smirk from spreading from heart to heart.

THE STUDENTS

Though the faculty grumble that the students majoring in business management are less capable and less well prepared than those majoring in other disciplines, the fact is that they meet the same admission criteria as do other students. Though the faculty complain that the students majoring in business management show considerably less interest than other students do in selecting electives in the arts and sciences, an examination of transcripts shows that they register for as many courses outside of their department as do the students in the liberal arts. What does distinguish these students from others, however, is the number of charges that they file. These range over a wide field, but the majority come to rest in two spots. One, no advising or poor advising. The faculty do not keep office hours; the faculty do not understand the general university requirements; the faculty do not care to help anyone. Two, no effective means of appeal. The chair is too busy to see students; when the chair does listen, he does not follow through; the chair could care less about students. Your executive secretary tells you that the chair's secretary has told him that you are not aware of one-third of the charges. Only the most aggressive and most sophisticated students write to you. Most feel that it is not worth the ink; nothing can be done anyway. No one can legislate caring. On four separate occasions in the past 2 years you have spoken to the chair at length about the need for reform. The number of complaints have not diminished, indeed, if anything they have increased. You have begun to hear from other chairs who have heard from their students that the wind chill index is uncomfortably low. The Department of Business Management has the worst retention rate on campus.

THE FACULTY

Of the 15 full-time faculty members in the Department of Business Management, only five are tenured and a more undistinguished group would not be easily assembled. Two possess D.B.A.s from research institutions, but are surly, malcontented refugees who had been exiled after a national firm's internal wars. A third earned his terminal degree from a nonaccredited university and defends rudeness and intimidation as methods that enhance learning. Numbers four and five, both in their late 50s, had taught for 30 years at a nearby religious college that had the year prior to the inauguration of this department collapsed under the weight of debts and mismanagement. Both had been looking for a rest home before applying for social security to finance exciting games of shuffleboard. All five have a number of characteristics in common: They are intellectually lethargic, but envious of those who are not; they are adept at avoiding work, but critical of those who are equally skillful; they dislike one another with zeal, but are perplexed when others share their discriminating taste. They hide their limited learning under bushels; they receive, with a fanfare of indignation, mediocre teaching evaluations; they are never sought for college committees and are a source of acrimony when they sit on departmental ones. They treat the 10 nontenured assistant professors who make up the rest of the full-time faculty in the department not as colleagues, but as junior apprentices unlikely to be granted a master's license.

The latter, uncomfortably aware that the five senior members of the department could at any time cut the rope that ties their dinghies to the mother ship now lean to cooperation now to rebellion and never in concert. Hence, the guerilla skirmishes are frequent and unhealthy. However, with no exception, the band of 10 is superior in all ways but experience to the band of five. Six of the 10 have come with Ph.D.s or D.B.A.s in pocket from highly respectable nearby institutions and the other four are A.B.D.s in the process of writing dissertations. All do reasonably well in the classroom; two are published; five are on retainers as industrial and business consultants. All want to remain in New England simply out of attachment to the area. They are inexperienced, naive, and frustrated, but energetic, good-natured, intellectually alive, and generally well intended. They have on occasion made common cause with the disproportionately large number of part-time faculty who come and go with little supervision and even less direction.

THE CHAIR

The chair, whose arrival on campus preceded yours by 3 years, has not had what baseball commentators in referring to pitchers call, "a quality start." A man of broad bureaucratic experience in governmental small business agencies, but of little understanding of the academic culture, he had moved with confidence and high style from blunder to blunder and had acquired in so doing a corroding level of animosity against his faculty—an animosity that he attempted to mask with excessive joviality. His drug of choice for all ills was a 2-hour luncheon at the local French bistro.

It had taken you less than a year in office to conclude tentatively that he had lost control of his department, or more likely, had never had it. However, your predecessor's recordkeeping would have shocked archivists, the tenured faculty in the department are unreliable witnesses, and you need time to disentangle facts from gossip in order to arrive at a fair judgment.

In a stepped-up effort to bypass the low road of internal strife and unglamorous tasks, the chair began to travel the high road of external public relations and fundraising. The time and energy that he increasingly devoted to cultivating the goodwill of the regional business community had not been without its rewards. He had acquired scholarship grants, an impressive number of unrestrictive gifts, many speaking engagements, and committee assignments on local charity drives.

Twice you have met with him, not over lunch, to make clear that the cultivation of goodwill among local business persons, however commendable, was not and should not be the highest item on his priority list. Neglect of scholarly matters and of academic standards could only lead to an ultimate lack of integrity. With great charm, he could not have agreed with you more. It was such a relief to him to be expected to support someone who shared his values. He repeated with conviction every point you made as if all of them had originated under his Vidal Sassoon haircut. You end each of the two meetings feeling as if you had been sprayed with honey. While you wash it off, students continue to complain and faculty singly and in small groups ask to see you. A Bartleby who "prefers to"?

You conclude that another attempt to communicate *viva voce* would serve no purpose and would likely result in his listening but not hearing. Hence, you attempt the written word.

Dear Chair:

It is my unpleasant responsibility to inform you that I have in the past 2 months received a number of visits and telephone calls from members of your faculty, some claiming to represent additional colleagues, who complained that the Department of Business Management was without direction in internal affairs. Specifically, they alleged that your office was merely a conduit for directives and suggestions from my office, that all academic enterprises were delegated—often to inexperienced faculty, and that no one could count on receiving guidance from you or working with you because you were so preoccupied with the outside community that you had never even bothered to learn the regulations that govern faculty and student matters.

If there is any merit to these very serious charges, you should recall my advice and explicit directives on several occasions when I stated unequivocally that no more than 10% of your time should be spent on work dealing with the off-campus community. Obviously, I would feel differently about the allocation of time if your department were in flawless academic order. As a reminder, I attach the document, "Responsibilities of the Department Chair," which the college reviews yearly. Please note that 12 of the 14 responsibilities relate to internal affairs.

Sincerely,

Within days you receive a reply.

Dear _____:

I agree with you. Ninety percent of my time should be spent attending to department matters. As you know, I am long on duties to perform and short on faculty to help me. So I have taken your advice seriously: I have not taken the time to attend a single event off campus in at least 2 months. I have been tied to this desk, and believe me, you will see progress soon.

If you wish to discuss this further, maybe we could meet for lunch. "Chez Fernande" is quiet and we could get a lot done away from campus.

Yours truly,

P.S. I may be wrong, but you seem to be taking all of this much too seriously. Smile and have a good day.

A week later, an anonymous well-wisher mails you the quarterly Chamber of Commerce News Summary. There through the yellow glow of a magic marker you learn that the chair has in the past 2 months been very active in a number of business enterprises and has just 2 weeks ago accepted the chairmanship of a Chamber of Commerce committee designed to help small local businesses.

The following day, as you wait for your blood pressure to return to normal, the five tenured members of the department vote 3 to 2 against renewing the contracts of the two assistant professors who publish, who teach well, and whose Ph.D.s were earned at fine universities. The reason? They judge them to be uncooperative.

SUGGESTED COURSE OF ACTION

Les jeux sont faits. Ask for the chair's resignation effective immediately.

Some 15, or perhaps even 20, years ago an otherwise undistinguished foreign film contained a memorable scene: A small industrialist in a French provincial town gave a yearly picnic for the heads of his departments. A long table covered in white linen sat on top of a knoll overlooking the wide expanse of the countryside and the town in the far distance. Some 30 persons dressed in their churchgoing best sat self-consciously on either side of the table when the industrialist sent word that the meal should begin without him. He had been unavoidably delayed and would join them shortly. They were well into the main course when the factory owner drove up in his limousine and approached the head of the table where an armchair awaited him. Everyone stood until he had sat. However, after sitting, instead of pulling his chair up to the table, the industrialist pulled the table up to him thereby causing 26 guests to reseat themselves before their neighbor's plate, 2 guests to reseat themselves without a table before them, and two plates filled with food to search for 2 missing guests. The next few minutes were filled with all 30 heads of departments trying to locate their half-eaten dinner rolls and their half-emptied wine glasses.

The scene was so inspired, so downright outrageous and funny that understanding the motives of the industrialist was at that moment beside the point. The act of monumental self-absorption stood there as a source of wonder. One looked at it the way one views a natural phenomenon. The chair's letter in response to yours is that sort of revealing act. To understand it fully would be to understand another fully, and in this case, such an other! Again, the provenance of such an act is not of the essence. For mundane or outré reasons, the chair is a compulsive yea-sayer to the point of lying.

In his *Essays*, Montaigne tells us, "If, like truth, the lie had but one face, we would be on better terms. For we would accept as certain the opposite of what the liar would say. But the reverse of truth has a hundred thousand faces and an infinite field." Hence, some philosophers despair of ever getting the "whole truth and nothing but the truth." That argument is relevant when referring to the complexity of the chair's behavior and the near impossibility of communicating with him. However, it does not apply when dealing with the one fact: when writing to you he chose to lie. No amount of speculating about the nature of truth and of his relation to it will change that. Your decision to act in all such cases should be restricted to considerations within the moral domain. To enter the epistemological one may well lead to paralysis.

Since you are now reasonably certain that no amount of patience or guidance is likely to bring about reform and that nothing less than reform is needed, you should immediately establish a search committee to replace the chair. That committee should include senior faculty from other departments to whom the seriousness of the need for change in the Department of Business Management has been made clear and from whom a pledge of commitment to help you solve what is ultimately a college problem you have received. The malaise and discord of a neighboring clan now threaten to cross disciplinary borders and to harm everyone. You most probably will even need to call an experienced senior faculty member from another department to serve as acting chair, for certainly no tenured professor in business is likely to restore order and no untenured faculty member is in a position to attempt to do so.

In its "Joint Statement on Government of Colleges and Universities" the American Association of University Professors recognizes that, "The President must at times, with or without support, infuse new life into a department." This is without a doubt one of those times. Out of courtesy to the five senior members of the Department of Business Management, you should ask them to meet with you privately for the purpose of outlining the decisions you have reached regarding their department. Schedule that meeting immediately before another you should call of the entire department. You want to avoid providing time between these two meetings for rumors and misinterpretations and anxieties to grow.

All concerned should be told in firm and unequivocal language that:

1. To enter faculty territory is a drastic act and that you wish to withdraw as soon as possible. You have consulted with the AAUP and College Senate leadership.
2. An acting chair has been named and a search committee established. Announce all names.
3. You will meet on a bi-monthly basis with the acting chair and will expect on those occasions to receive a progress report on objectives, which he will establish with them subject to your approval.
4. Appointment, reappointment, promotion, and tenure decisions will continue to be subject to the recommendation of the tenured faculty.
5. You are, however, appointing two senior faculty from other departments to act as advisers and observers on all such matters. Name them. They should both have wide experience in traditional academic questions and be highly respected in the college.
6. These two observers will be present at every meeting of faculty search committees and promotion, tenure, and reappointment committees and will also attend appropriate departmental meetings. They will have the consulting services of a senior faculty member who teaches business management at a nearby university.
7. The two advisers will submit to you a written report every 3 months.
8. You will expect a 5-year staffing plan on your desk within 6 months, after the new chair is named.
9. You fully expect that this department will meet the same professional and academic criteria as do all others.

Regardless of the pressures placed on you by persons or time do not dismantle any of these supports until you are absolutely certain that the house will stand alone. The decisive action you have taken should come as a relief to the senior faculty in the department, who probably at some level realize that they live in a house of cards and are secretly pleased that you have set up wind screens. It should also be welcomed by the junior faculty, who have had to feel very threatened and who have been in no position to put up protective coverings. However, it is essential that decisive action be successful the first time around when strength can be respected because it appears to be informed by intelligence and wisdom. The need for a second or third attempt to correct this kind of situation can only be interpreted at best as well-intended muddling. The chances of hitting the target will actually decrease with every shot of an arrow.

Finally, you should seek every opportunity to name members of the business management faculty to college-wide committees so that they begin to feel some dedication to the enterprise as a whole; so that they begin to understand the academic culture by working with others who presumably know it better than they do; so that members of the community at large may begin to seek a rapprochement with colleagues whose orientation may be slightly different from their own. Simultaneously, you must find ways to encourage the business management department faculty to develop a sense of pride and loyalty toward the smaller unit to which they belong and which in a very real sense can to the benefit of them all become a professional home.

Few, even in academe, outgrow the primitive need to belong to a discrete group.

CHAPTER SIX

THE LITTLE ENGINE
THAT MIGHT

A CASE OF COMMUNITY SERVICE

An academician whose home university stands in gothic and stained glass splendor in the pit of an American ghetto with demoralizing crime statistics is fond of repeating the following anecdote as a parable of a contemporary dilemma. Though violence in the public schools throughout the university's far-flung neighborhood had often crouched behind lockers and waited for victims in empty classrooms, and though both teachers and pupils had long since resignedly accommodated to its menace, a series of recent shootings had driven even the most submissive and the most fatalistic to cry for help. In the space of a month five 14 and 15 year olds had used Saturday night specials to settle arguments over basketball jackets and baseball cards. On three separate occasions, in three separate settings, our academic raconteur was asked in a tone that left no doubt that all three questioners expected an answer, "What is the university doing about this?"

American public colleges/universities as opposed to German, French, and British ones have a fairly long history of "doing something about this." Ever since Congress passed the Morrill Act, in 1862, land grant institutions, especially in the Midwest and Far West, have rarely behaved as if good fences made good neighbors. For over 100 years these colleges/universities have taught the farmer how to raise better crops, the cattle rancher how to take care of his ailing steer, the housewife how to bake and store foods, and the lonely youngster how to speak to Homer. This dedication to community and government involvement and service, which had not characterized private higher education before World War II, took on from roughly the mid-1940s a glamour and an allurement that few colleges/universities, large or small, public or private, have either tried or been able to resist. Government, at all levels, corporations, and foundations have offered money to the greedy, fame to the proud, flattery to the insecure, travel to the restless, power to the ambitious, and even rest to the weary.

There is no denying that as a result of all these blandishments, academics, especially scientists and social scientists, have exerted considerable influence in both the public and private domains and have shared knowledge, discoveries, and insights with those who wield economic and political power to the greater good, in many instances, of the general population. However, fraternization with business, government, and foundations as one of the purposes of the college/university has not been and is not without its critics.

Traditionalists, such as Jacques Barzun and Sidney Hook, have argued that colleges/universities best serve the greater community by devoting their talent and energies to scholarship and teaching inspired by their own muse. Let society then acquire part of the interest from the growing capital. Ironically, not a few of the reformers from Columbia to Berkeley in the early 1970s would have agreed that many an academician had become a soldier of corporate or government fortune, jetting from city to city shooting at problems targeted by CEOs in Manhattan's glass towers or Washington's mock royal palaces. Nearly 30 years ago Jacques Barzun warned that on an American campus, "Pleasure and prestige alike depend on being away as often and as long as possible" (*The House of Intellect*, Harper & Row, New York, 1959, p. 193).

The dimension of an institution's struggle with the nature and form of its service to the community outside its walls will depend in great part on its size, its type, and its special mission. It will quite obviously take much less effort to bring the matter's shoulders to the mat in a small private liberal arts college than in a multiversity with its institutes and think tanks and special-purpose centers and numerous internationally acclaimed faculty. In his Godkin Lectures, delivered at Harvard University, in 1963, Clark Kerr even then described the University of California as having

> a total employment of over 40,000 people . . . operations in over a hundred locations, counting campuses, experiment stations, agricultural and urban extension centers, and projects abroad involving more than fifty countries; nearly 10,000 courses in its catalogues; some form of contact with nearly every industry, nearly every level of government, nearly every person in its region. (*The Uses of The University*, Harper & Row, New York, 1963, p. 7)

An American who has crossed his country's prairies, climbed its mountain ranges, and sailed its rivers will accept a theory that claims that small is beautiful *contre coeur*. Many an American administrator who is told that the University of California is the world's largest purveyor of white mice secretly whispers Mary Lou Retton's "watch out, big boys."

THE BACKGROUND

In a historically underfunded public institution in a section of the country where it appears that private is often admired simply for not being public, you have days when you suspect that there may be few trees left to cut in the cherry orchard. Your Chekhovian metaphor is pure self-indulgence, for your college sprawls on 20 acres of an urban ghetto that has made you street-wise and feisty. In a word, you have mastered survival skills.

When, for example, demographics projected a precipitous decline in the number of local and regional high school graduates and the specter of retrenchment threatened to demoralize your faculty, you led a committee that established an effective marketing plan. This plan had as its hub a concerted effort to encourage the newly arrived foreign-born and their children from Korea, Vietnam, and Communist bloc countries who had settled in the city to enroll as part-time and full-time degree-seeking students. The plan had worked better than even the optimists had predicted and for several years your enrollment has hovered around 4,200 FTES.

However, success nearly always rings for room service soon after its arrival. The traditional remedial reading and writing English courses established some 15 years ago that have had some effect in preparing native-born students to do college level work prove too weak a prescription for a member of the bright but foreign-speaking Vietnamese boat-people and Russian Jewish immigrants. Consequently, you established 5 years ago an English Language Center, which is now staffed with a small faculty whose specialty is the teaching of English as a second language, which operates day and evening year round, which is well equipped with language laboratories, and which allows the foreign-born of college age to take intensive courses in listening, speaking, reading, and writing. Students are admitted to the college once the director of the center has verified their English language proficiency.

The center, enormously popular, has become the social hub of the international student set. Its exotic monthly parties featuring a talk on some feature of the culture of a foreign land and a sampling of appropriate foreign dishes has attracted the American students who covet invitations, and enrollment in foreign language classes and international studies have had a modest but cheering growth. The students' immigrant parents are touchingly grateful, the retention rate among the foreign students themselves is very high, and the college is somewhat less provincial than it had been before the establishment of the center. All causes for rejoicing.

THE HAPPENING

The newly appointed president of the City School Board, Mr. P., is a blustery, well-intended, controversial activist given to pronouncements of staggering simplicity. Complexity, according to his world view, is the refuge of the timid, and patience a mask worn by cowards. He always chooses, like the citizens of Lake Wobegon, to get up and do. He makes for lively copy and attracts many who would agree that this particular city school system is among those that place our nation at risk. After 12 years of schooling, all too often Johnny cannot read or write or compute. Parents are bewildered, employers are outraged, and students are both embarrassed and vaguely aware that they should probably consider suing somebody.

At his first press conference, Mr. P. described the situation as "a damn disgrace that this great city was sick of." He intended with all the authority vested in him to plant his spurs "into the sides of several jackasses." No, he would not name the donkeys now, but he was certainly prepared to so later if "they didn't jump after being spiked." The public school system of this fine city had made him what he was today and the taxpayers could from this day on count on getting a decent return on their money.

OCTOBER 22—10:00 A.M.
Mr. P. is on the line and wishes to speak to you.

"Hello, how are you, young lady?"

"Fine, Mr. P. How are you?"

"Why, if I were any better, I'd have to be hospitalized. You don't mind my calling you 'young lady'?"

"Well, it's done. Congratulations on your new appointment."

"Thank you. I saw you at the breakfast following my press conference. Someone pointed you out to me. Aren't you too small to be a dean? How do you handle all these football players?"

After several minutes of such backslapping hearty brotherhood-of-moose-lodge humor, you learn that Mr. P. wants to go into business with you. He has been reading about how universities and school systems should cooperate, and one of his aides has come up with an idea that he likes very much and that he is sure you will like also. Since there is no time to lose, would you meet him for lunch the day after tomorrow? Surely. You would be pleased to do so.

During the course of this meal, beneath Mr. P.'s tiresome manners and rhetoric, you discover a proposal worthy of serious consideration. The success of your English Language Center has not escaped the notice of the City School Board members, and Mr. P. would like you to extend its services to include minority youths in the public school system. In sum he would like you to establish and to finance a pilot project for 20 ninth-grade students from the nearest high school 3 miles away from the campus. These students would attend classes for two 2-hour sessions a week after the regular school day and would be taken on field trips to cultural events in the city. Each year an additional ninth-grade group would be added so that in the fourth year of the plan 80 students from the ninth through the twelfth grades would participate in this program of enrichment. Since mastery of language is the *sine qua non* of academic success, the hope is that at the end of 4 years these students would read, speak, and write well enough to begin college with confidence and to earn a baccalaureate degree in 4 years.

You are open, but guarded for two reasons: one, the success of such an enterprise would depend upon the generosity and enthusiasm of those who would implement it and you have long since understood the foolishness of attempting to impose either; and, two, your discretionary funds have never matched the university's goodwill. Mr. P. detects your caution and misinterprets it as his version of an intellectual's typical avoidance of quick and

decisive action. He pockets your promise to investigate the pos-
sibilities of initiating such a project, but he gives signs of not being
in the habit of receiving less than assurances in return for lunch
at his posh club.

At this time of the year faculty are neck deep into midterm
examinations and committee agenda items that had been proposed
in the invigorating air of the opening of the academic term when
no stream appeared too deep to ford. Since the success of any
undertaking depends in part on timing, you have always avoided
calling for a redistribution of efforts in the middle of a semester
when most faculty have already set both their sights and their
clocks. However, the neighboring school is in great need; Mr. P.'s
request is a dramatic but real appeal to save lives; Mr. P. and his
colleagues are influential both in the city's and in the state's political chambers.

At the end of the following week, you discuss the matter with
the director of the English Language Center, Dr. Y., a middle-
aged, no-nonsense work-horse whose biyearly reports inevitably
admonish the university for asking too much and giving too little.
"If the university cares about its international and immigrant students, it will . . ." has become her ritualistic opening when urging
the adoption of any course of action. Her response in this case
could have been anticipated: she is unenthused, not out of cal-
lousness or apathy, but out of anxiety over an overburdened faculty and staff and undernourished budget. However, she sees the
need of considering the proposal with care. She will meet with
her faculty and staff, a dedicated group nearly wholly responsible
for the success of the center, and will prepare a recommendation
for you as soon as possible.

Two weeks go by during which time you tend the fires that
should burn and put out those that should not. You then leave
for a 3-day out-of-state national meeting of the American Council
on Education. In digging through the telephone messages taken
by your secretary in your absence, you come upon one from Mr.
P.'s executive secretary. Would you please call him immediately.
The matter, of course, is urgent.

Mr. Executive Secretary's tone is that of a young man on the
rise: a combination of unctuousness and peremptoriness. The
square jaw and the firmly mounted subdued Dior tie comes right
over the telephone lines. Mr. P. was so pleased by your supportive
response to his proposal. Of course, it has been nearly a month
since you met for lunch, and he did expect to hear from you sooner

than this. However, he does understand that professors grind their corn slowly. But so as not to lose time, both he and Mr. P. met with the principal of the targeted high school and he is happy to report that Principal H. is very excited about the plan. As a matter of fact, he is hoping that you will meet with him very soon so as to begin working out the details. Principal H. as well as Mr. P. are both convinced that the university never intended to pay the city's native minority students less attention than that given the recently arrived minority youngsters. He certainly hopes that you have a most pleasant Thanksgiving holiday. It must be difficult for a woman who holds down your job to cook meals with all the trimmings. His wife, who prefers not to work, has said often that she certainly could not manage it. After you hang up, you indulge in the formulation of several witty but devastating Miss Manners lines too impolitic to use even if you had been quick enough to invent them on the spot.

The Monday after Thanksgiving carries with it another turn of the screw: a call from Principal H. The latter, a sweet yes-man whose slouching toward retirement has been obvious to many for some time, is clearly nervous and distraught. While the rumor that he escapes the barbarisms of his inner city school by locking himself in his office and listening to Vivaldi may be exaggerated, there can be no doubt that he is less than eager to be tapped for a difficult mission 2 years before an honorable discharge. There can also be no doubt that saying even a soft "no" to Mr. P. could turn out to be a lonely adventure. Of course, it is a splendid idea and he certainly wishes that it could work. But how is he to find 20 ninth-graders who would be willing to go to school after hours when truant officers cannot manage to keep them in school during hours? Who would then ask these youngsters to forego for 4 years sports and clubs and other activities that take place after the regular school day? What about transportation? Maybe Mr. P.'s vision includes suburban station wagons with leaping shaggy dogs? And what happens in the third and fourth year when the youngsters lose out on part-time evening work? And who is expected to per-suade the parents? Do you and Mr. P. not realize that he works in a world where he cannot keep a print on the wall and a coffee pot in the lounge? By the time Principal H. finds himself spinning about in the vortex of nonsequiturs, you can only sympathize and assure him that the project was being carefully studied on campus and had not even reached a stage where you judged it practicable. For that reason, you had not called him. Should the director of the university's English Language Center and her faculty and staff conclude that the idea was worth pursuing, then, of course, you would ask to meet with him to see if he were prepared to undertake the venture. Principal H. apologizes for his excitability, but he is under constant pressure. Mr. P. is certainly a very fine man and he cannot imagine anyone better suited to preside over the City School Board. We have needed his kind of vigorous leadership for a long time. He for one will cooperate in every way he can. You assure him not only that you understand but that you will keep this conversation confidential.

That same day the director of the center informs you that she will need one more week before submitting a written detailed recommendation. She and her faculty and staff are examining every aspect of the proposal, for she has always agreed with your conviction that we should not undertake anything that we cannot do well. However, she can tell you right now that the members s of the center are evenly divided between those who are willing to establish this proposed branch to the center if certain conditions are met (details to follow) and those who would ask not to be associated with this departure from the original mission of the center. The reasons supporting both positions will form part of the forthcoming report.

The Sunday edition of the city's major newspaper contains a picture of the mayor, the chair of the City Council, the superintendent of schools, and Mr. P., held hands upraised, declaring war on mediocrity in the public school system.

Two days later you receive the director of the center's report, which is signed by all four full-time, two part-time faculty members, and two staff members.

Dear _____:

After long hours of debate, the final vote on the question of expanding the mission of the English Language Center to include instruction for youngsters of high school age as proposed by Mr. P. was: Aye - 4; Nay - 4. A hung jury is as satisfying as a tie ballgame and we understand that you are still left with a difficult decision to make. While a decision reached by consensus would still have been only advisory, advice supported by shared conviction is at least something upon which you might have leaned. As it is, the convictions of the faculty will neither "see nor saw"; the weight is equally distributed.

Since I voted with the Nay's, let me begin by summarizing the attitude of those who believe that we should pursue this course. I want the last word before the curtain falls. In their view, the cost for the first year's operation would be fairly modest. A projected one year budget might look something like this:

Direct Costs
Personnel
  Salary and Wages

a.	Coordinator (300 hours × $10/hr)	$3,000
b.	Teacher (120 class hours × $20/hr)	2,400
c.	Secretary (300 hrs × $5.75/hr)	1,725
d.	Teaching assistant	600
	subtotal	$7,725

Fringe Benefits
  FICA—7.15% × 5,400 (a + b above) $ 386

Other Costs

Books (20 students × $65)	$1,300
Supplies	2,000
Brochure/mailing/newsletter	500
Transportation to and from the university	2,000
Field trips (2–3 per year)	500
Evaluation materials	600
subtotal	$6,900

Indirect Costs
  Negotiated approved rate on campus—
    61% of all salaries and wages $4,712
           TOTAL $19,723

Costs Assumed by the University
  Tickets to on- and off-campus
    cultural/sporting events ($800)

The university might find a sponsor for the first year of operation and simultaneously seek long-term support for a budget that would obviously quadruple in 4 years without taking inflation into account. What else could we do that might actually save human lives at the cost of roughly $1,000 per student per year?

In the view of the yea-sayers, this is an opportunity to reach out to those in need; to establish communication with a neighboring public school system in a way that might lead to further cooperative efforts; to make strong political allies; to dispel the myth that the campus is isolated, snobbish, and uncaring. Hence, we pass Go if we can find the needed funds.

The objections of those who oppose the move, and I count myself among them, wish you and others to understand that we are not callous before the needs of youngsters who might well benefit by participating in such a plan and we are not indifferent to the potential consequences of denying them access to the center. We are, however, convinced that the success of the ELC has been in great part due to its clear, strong, stable identity and that to assume an added personality would precipitate schizophrenia. In addition to this gloomy forecast, we would list certain practical considerations that in themselves should give us pause. In speaking with you, Principal H. has already referred to several, which you have shared with us, but no one has yet mentioned insurance coverage in transporting these 20, then 40, then 60, then 80 high school students to and from the high school; the safety of these same students who would have to walk home at night after being dropped off at the high school following classes at the center; the criteria for choosing the youngsters in the first place; the special training for faculty only prepared to teach college-level students.

I realize that the above has the tone of a lament, but the world is not always user friendly. Sorry.

If you would like to discuss all or any of this, I'm at your disposal.

Sincerely,

Dr. Y.
Director of the ELC

SUGGESTED COURSE OF ACTION

Turn down, with regret, Mr. P.'s request. If you have heart and imagination, you find it easier to resist evil than to resist good. Indeed, you may even find it difficult to admit of circumstances under which one should say no to another's need. However, in such instances, the question to be answered is not the one most often asked, namely, "Is it worth doing?" but, rather, "Should we be the ones to do it?" Of course, the poor should be fed, the sick visited, and the ignorant educated. But the world's labor is wisely divided into very special functional units so that an institution's energies may be greatly amplified by remaining properly focused.

Though you have an ELC faculty that has proved itself to be very effective in dealing with foreign adults who are presumably self-propelled and desirous of mastering English so as to be admitted to university classes and to succeed once having been admitted, you are without the slightest evidence that this same faculty would succeed in teaching and motivating inner-city youngsters who would have to be persuaded that this medicine might cure a disease whose existence they are apt to deny. Furthermore, one half of the faculty, including the director of the center, has judged the project unwise. To impose it on them and thereby to redistribute the use of their time by fiat is almost certain to cause resentment, to lower morale, and to damage a unit of your institution that by all accounts is engaged in doing very fine and very appropriate work. One might add that you have no guarantee of funding, that in 4 years the cost of the project for a university of your type would be substantial, and that even if the enterprise proved less than spectacularly successful, ending it after a period of time might well attract more moles to your lawn than not undertaking it in the first place.

Saying no to Mr. P. will most probably prove to be as pleasant as severe whiplash and its effects as long lasting. However, you must not allow yourself to be intimidated by those in high places nor bullied by references to the race of inner-city youngsters. You should meet with him and explain why you have decided as you have and attempt to make clear that it is not to the taxpayers' or to the public school system's or to your university's best interests for the ELC to duplicate what is, after all, the local high school's mission. The faculty of the center would, however, be pleased to share knowledge and materials with the public school teachers who might be interested in the very special methodologies of teaching English as a second language.

The recent calls for colleges/universities to help schools bring about reform are in part a response to the conclusions drawn by the dozens of national and state commissions charged directly or indirectly with an investigation of the following mystery. Why cannot Johnny and Janie after 12 years of instruction write and speak English effectively nor understand an essay in a scientific journal written for laymen? After inspecting the house, the detectives posted large danger signs.

One might recall with profit that attempts to institute cooperative ventures between the public schools and higher education are not the yield of recently planted arbors. Vintners can celebrate a centennial of efforts, but few vintage years. In 1884, the president of Harvard, Charles Eliot, founded a "Committee of Ten" to promote cooperation among school and college teachers and to encourage reform. Since then the ventures, like all community service ventures, have yielded mixed results and can now only be characterized as high risk. And risk taking may or may not be commendable depending on the circumstances.

One might also guard against misunderstanding the argument between those who would set up soup kitchens and those who would insist on spending the time doing research on nutrition. It is not a simple-minded human affair where one camp is generous and the other self-absorbed. Those on both sides of the issue wish to serve the community. The question that they answer differently is *how* does one best serve.

All proposed faculty-run community service projects might be asked to take the following test before being approved.

1. Is the project in keeping with the academic mission of the college/university? Will it detract from it?
2. Are the faculty, as a class by and large oriented toward theory and not practice, the ones best suited to undertake this project?
3. Did faculty initiate the proposal and thereby give promise of commitment and enthusiasm?
4. Will the time and resources given to this project cause the neglect of more important ones?
5. Are the time and resources given to this project apt to be cut off or substantially reduced within a period short enough to cause resentment?
6. Do the promotion, tenure, and merit pay policies of your institution allow you to reward the faculty who will undertake this project?

Something in man leads good quarterbacks to open poor restaurants.

CHAPTER SEVEN

OÙ SONT LES NEIGES D'ANTAN?

A CASE OF OUTSIDE EMPLOYMENT

I have heard of a woman who preferred to ski when the visibility was near zero so that she would not see where she was plunging. Among the many trails that administrators might be tempted to avoid if they could see where they led, the one marked "Faculty Outside Employment" is treacherous even for experts. However, on both clear and foggy days in ever increasing numbers department chairs, deans, and academic vice-presidents are pushed onto it and reach the lodge more or less battered.

No one argues that a full-time job merits less than full-time effort, but reaching consensus on a definition of "full time" is far more challenging than the uninitiated might believe. Faculty workloads and outside employment, matters that were once left quite comfortably to the ethical standards and general goodwill of administrators and faculty alike, should now according to some be dealt with in the most precise of terms. As student enrollments and budgets diminish, state agencies and governing boards demand greater accountability and college/university administrators seek higher productivity. Simultaneously, faculty in an attempt to supplement an income that has not kept up with inflation and wishing to pursue the many opportunities for consulting and research in business and industry view themselves as free agents and independent scholars.

Whether one's view of the American soul corresponds to Tocqueville's image as generous and gregarious or to D. H. Lawrence's as hard and isolate; or whether one sees this soul as constantly divided within itself in wishing now to build communities, now to build sanctuaries; or whether one is persuaded that this once unselfish soul has become self-absorbed, it may be both enlightening and useful to place the contemporary professors' "habits of the heart" within context.

The American mythical hero has died alone on prairies, lived alone near ponds, fought alone on whalers, and when life became too crowded lit out alone for territories. And any two nights before a television set will reveal the American contemporary hero as standing alone in corrupt courtrooms, struggling alone to expose ill-intended cartels, and working alone to save the widow's mortgaged ranch. Americans may join the Kiwanians, but they dream of winning a gold medal in some individual event.

Given the cultural penchant toward individualism, given that associations of professionals from medieval guilds to modern colleges/universities are a result in part of enlightened self-interest, one might be appropriately skeptical of conclusions that describe the contemporary faculty's commitment to a community of scholars on 227 acres of land in Boston or Toledo as more fragile than that of his predecessors. It may well be that the configurations of an American scholar's neighborhood have always been defined by intellectual interest and not by geography. That is, when he left his study long enough to walk through the neighborhood.

Of course, anyone's position in this debate will be influenced by his remembrance of the snows of yesteryear and the kind of institution to which he refers. The theme is played in a different key in research universities as opposed to comprehensive universities, in colleges of liberal arts as opposed to community colleges.

> "Twenty years ago a faculty member would have chaired an important committee without expecting a reduction in his teaching load."

> "Twenty years ago a faculty member would have been working in the university's chemistry laboratory whereas now he spends his time in some industrial bio-tech laboratory across town."

> "Twenty years ago a faculty member spent a Tuesday in October raking the leaves off his lawn and now he spends it giving advice to local CPA firms."

The trail is indeed difficult, and remembering Natty Bumppo and Sam Spade as one takes its twists and turns is not only great fun but even likely upon occasion to prevent a fall.

THE BACKGROUND

Your midwestern, private, multipurpose university (FTES 9,000) offers a mix of programs in the arts and sciences and professional degrees in business, law, pharmacy, and computer sciences. Your campus fortuitously located on the northern edge of a sleepy city (population 175,000) borders the southern portion of vital suburbs that have tripled in size in the past 10 years. Two high technology and bio-technology parks have grown even beyond the optimistic forecasting of their developers. Since meeting your enrollment predictions has always meant attracting a significant number of commuters, you have shared in this suburban success. The sons and daughters of the newly arrived professionals are registering as full-time students, and the professionals themselves, as well as their husbands and wives, are attending evening and weekend courses. Other benefits have accrued: Some of the scientists and engineers are teaching for you part time; the companies are contributing to your scholarship fund and hiring your alumni. Your relationship with the CEOs of the various firms, while not a marriage of true minds, is cordial, supportive, and pleasant.

THE HAPPENING

Associate professor M., who was awarded tenure 6 years ago, is a bright, energetic, early middle-aged professional whose creative papers have already contributed more to his field than has the limited research of his senior colleagues. The jealousy aroused by this success is tempered by Professor M.'s personality, which appears to be genuinely outgoing and generous. He clings not only to the style, plaid shirts, chinos, boots, granny glasses, and a pony tail, of his former flower-child self, but to the manner, gentle, nonthreatening, and amused, idealized over discussions of Camus and Kierkegaard in university coffee shops across the land some 25 years ago. He advises students; he is flexible about his teaching schedule; and though he avoids committee work he has recently compensated for that lapse by initiating the following project.

Two years ago, with the approval of the chair of the Department of Mathematics, Dr. M. had established an applied mathematics laboratory designed to challenge the university's senior mathematics majors with problems similar to those that they might be asked to solve as in-house mathematicians in business and industry. Under contract and for a small fraction of the cost of professional consultants, firms within the region could request the students who directed this laboratory under Dr. M.'s supervision to conduct various studies. Within months a dozen majors were attempting to improve the efficiency in testing of an electronic repair center and to increase the speed of transmitting checks from branch banks to a central office. While no one was surprised that Dr. M. had hit a homerun, many wondered why he had come to the plate at all. They had not expected him to play in a game of profit and loss; they had thought his interest in numbers to have been of a totally different nature. But then, he had always been a giving sort who cared about the future of his students and surely he had been inspired by a desire to help them rather than by a sudden and uncharacteristic urge to seek rapprochement with stock gazers. At any rate, the enterprise seemed intellectually sound and in keeping with the mission of your institution, so you had written him a note of approval and gratitude.

The Sunday edition of the city newspaper runs a half-page story with colored photographs in praise of what it terms a model cooperative effort between businesses that have been important contributors to the community and a university that has in the past few years shown signs of wanting to end its isolation.

Well, the Fates' clear, consistent, and finally overwhelming preference for Dr. M. over all other mathematicians in the department and perhaps even over those in the entire state awakens the Salieri in a singularly unproductive full professor who wants certain of Dr. M.'s activities investigated and tells the chair of the department so in writing. He has it on very good authority that Dr. M. lives in the same world we all do after all: His interest in numbers is particularly acute when they adorn federal reserve notes. In direct violation of the university's regulations limiting outside consulting to 1 day a week, Dr. M., having profited from the contacts he had made as supervisor of the Applied Mathematics Laboratory, had been working for an artificial intelligence firm in the evenings and on certain hours of many weekdays. Word was that he had even been provided an office on the top floor of the company's central building and that he had been seen walking in and out of the building on numerous occasions on weekends. All this while other faculty, without recognition from either top administrators or the press, carried the burdens of an underfunded department. Dr. M., it was clear, had never cared about the university but only about himself and possibly about his discipline. He for one was sick of it and looking forward to retirement. If he were younger and his wife were not ill, he might even leave to go teach elsewhere. Incidentally, he had heard that Dr. M. was seen wearing a suit when entering the firm's offices on weekdays. He cannot be certain of that, but his witnesses are reliable. At any rate, you may read into this dress for success behavior what you will; he has drawn his own conclusions.

Several days later when asked to describe both the extent and the nature of his outside employment, Dr. M.'s response reflects the self-confidence upon which his energetic but gentle manner is grounded.

Dear Dr. Z.:

I will of course meet with you at the appointed time early next week to discuss my work at Artificial Intelligence Inc. However, it might be useful for you to consider certain facts before we talk. That way, we can both come in prepared.

I have for the past 18 months worked as a consultant in the computer security division of Artificial Intelligence Inc. The number of hours a week which I've given to this company's projects has varied over the months. Normally, I've gone in every Wednesday afternoon and two or three evenings a week. These hours when combined have averaged one day a work week as permitted by university regulations.

I have, however, also worked frequently on weekends on these same projects at the firm's headquarters for two reasons. I've been given a small private office and the use of a computer far more sophisticated than anything we have at the university. The combination is very enticing to someone who for the past 13 years has had to share an office in the department with another faculty member and who for the past 6 to 7 years has had to think across the beat of soft rock played on my two sons' stereos.

The work I do for this firm is clearly of some value and I get paid for it. However, am I not free to spend my weekends as I like? Would anyone be questioning me if I spent Saturdays lifting weights and Sundays fishing? And what if I won prize money doing the first and sold the fish to local markets? I'm not being entirely facetious, because my work as a mathematician has always been my recreation and my passion. The university pays me for doing it during the normal work week and a business firm pays me for doing it on weekends.

If I were neglecting my duties at the university, I could understand your concerns. However, the evaluation of my teaching and advising is among the highest in the department, my research has been ranked superior (though I want to discuss this point with you when we meet), and the time I give to the Applied Mathematics Laboratory exceeds that required of those working on any committee.

I hope that the tone of this letter is neither defensive nor whining. It was not meant to be. My only purpose in writing it was to give you an opportunity to see the matter from my perspective before we met.

One last point. The paper I published last month and the one that is now in press were both based on work which I had done originally though in different form for Artificial Intelligence Inc.

Sincerely,

M.

The meeting between the chair of the department and Dr. M. is cordial and honest and reveals one additional motive for the latter's attachment to his consulting work. At 46, he has become convinced that his contributions to his specialization while very solid had never been spectacular and are probably now at an end. He has, however, lost neither his love of nor his zeal for his discipline and senses the possibility of a renewal that could propel him into significant work were he now to redirect his energies into the application of certain theories. The consulting work, while not the exclusive means of reaching that destination, was certainly a fast and comfortable one. The publications and professional papers that he was certain to write would, of course, redound to the university's reputation.

Since the matter has become one of debate both within and without the Department of Mathematics, the chair refers it to a higher court and asks you to rule. He, however, given his love of precision and definite solutions, leans toward a strict interpretation of the rules. True, the regulation in question simply refers to outside employment being limited to "1 day a week" as opposed to "1 day a calendar week." However, long usage and custom had accepted as implied that in such cases the university intended calendar week and not work week. After all, were we to begin encouraging faculty to sell insurance and Amway products on weekends? Of course, if Dr. M. were not getting paid, things might be different. He has one faculty member whose service to the community consists of keeping the books for the local Methodist church. The important thing to bear in mind is that our decision in these cases should encourage not dissuade dedication to the university. If faculty want to work weekends, there is plenty to be done for the department and its students.

SUGGESTED COURSE OF ACTION

If upon investigation you conclude that Dr. M. is a productive scholar, a well-respected teacher, and a responsible colleague, buy him a glass of Chablis and seek his advice on faculty development. For what would be gained by insisting that Dr. M. spend his Sunday afternoons in his campus office instead of his firm's office when the results of his research adds to the university's reputation and is supportive of its mission. This professor's sense of self-worth and mature directing of energies are fueled by the passion he has maintained for his discipline. To frustrate that passion for any but grave cause is at best unwise and at worst revelatory of a questionable hierarchy of values.

If the chair of the Department of Mathematics is correct in maintaining that by tradition the university's regulation that states that a faculty member may devote only 1 day a week to outside consulting has been interpreted to mean 1 day per calendar week, and if that tradition is to be continued, then the regulation should be rewritten to say precisely what the university intends. However, what purpose would be served by limiting your flexibility with a rule whose language is more restrictive than the one that now exists? Dr. M.'s conduct is not in violation of professional ethics, is not abusive of faculty privilege, and is not in conflict with his institutional responsibilities.

Perhaps you fear, as does the chair of the mathematics department, that a liberal interpretation of the rules governing outside employment will encourage faculty less enthused about their discipline than Dr. M. is to spend time on weekends if not during the work week in commercial enterprises unrelated to their obligations as professors. While that fear is not unwarranted, you can reduce the danger of your faculty's becoming part-time real-estate developers by writing a position paper on the responsibilities of full-time faculty, having it reviewed by the faculty leadership, and asking that each faculty member who intends to engage in outside consulting, research, or teaching report the nature and extent of these activities to the chair of his department so that together they may weigh them on the scales that your generous, supportive, but firm directives have provided. Some will claim that weekends are beyond your jurisdiction. Fine, but judging the accomplishments and contributions of a full-time faculty member is not. Neither is determining just rewards and meting out just sanctions.

Perhaps you fear walking through the jungle unprotected by a thick shield of precise and detailed regulations when you know attorneys to be lurking behind bushes and bargaining agents and AAUP personnel sitting in the crooks of trees. There is no question that eyes mark your passage and that you should take care not to trip on surface roots. However, the courts have already determined that a university is within its rights in limiting outside work for its faculty and in defining what conforms with its educational standards. In *Gross* v. *University of Tennessee* (1978, 1980) the court held that two tenured professors in the health sciences had "no constitutional right to engage in the unlimited private practice of medicine while holding a public position of employment." The court further held that "the income limiting agreements utilized were rationally related to the espoused legitimate goals of fostering full-time devotion to teaching duties." In *Stastny* v. *Board of Trustees of Central Washington University* a tenured professor of history who defied administrative directives by traveling to a foreign conference to present a paper when he should have helped at registration and met his students at the opening days of classes was found to have been justly dismissed. In the court's judgment, "academic freedom is not a license for activity at variance with job related procedures and requirements, nor does it encompass activities which are internally destructive to the proper function of the university . . ." In addition, the AAUP while as careful as we should all be to protect the rights of faculty recognizes in its policy documents and reports the need to impose both minor and major sanctions on the few who behave unprofessionally and irresponsibly.

Perhaps you fear being accused of allowing Dr. M. to be paid twice for doing the work once. Avoid developing the habits of mind of a good auditor. The account sheets must balance, of course, but one does not reach the bottom line in a university the way one reaches it in a razor blade factory. Even in a postindustrial age you will not persuade the general public that a professor's contributions cannot be measured with a time clock, but any attempt to copy business and industrial means of assessing productivity will quickly find you dancing on hot coals. In the case of Dr. M., no deception is involved; the technical firm apparently considers its investment in him a good one; the university is more than pleased with his performance; and the work being done is directly related to Dr. M.'s scholarly interests. If a mathematician's discoveries cannot accept funds from industry, what will an English professor do with the royalties for a novel written on weekends and holidays? And what of the advance mailed in anticipation of the finished manuscript?

Perhaps you fear and resent Dr. M.'s suspected lack of total commitment to the university. If he were entirely and selflessly devoted to his department and to his students, would he seek outside opportunities? Would he not spurn nonacademics who seek to distract him from the campus's causes? Such questions remind me of my favorite parish school jokes: the apocryphal story about the headline of a diocesan paper which read, "Few Catholics Drown in Flood." Only if you need parochial dreams should you worry about how dedicated the players are to the uniforms they wear. Your responsibility and that of Dr. M. is not limited to preserving, sharing, and discovering knowledge for the benefit of the few who call themselves your students, but extends to all who seek to know. For the temporal conveniences of funding and management we assign ourselves space and duties; for the attractive challenges of competitive play, we attempt to upstage one another, but the vision we all share is to feed everyone who hungers. That is the ultimate reason for supporting a Dr. M. and for setting aside all fears of doing so as pusillanimous.

An attempt to define "full time" as in "full-time faculty" will be as successful as an attempt to define poetry. While there are a thousand and one definitions of a poem, no one can agree on the adequacy of any single statement. Hence, everyone has come to settle for being able to recognize a poem. In the same way, a university can recognize its full-time faculty with ease and should defend them against unreasonable external controls and protect them from excessive internal restraints. Only under such conditions will all of your individualistic scholars think of themselves as forming a spiritual community that deserves their allegiance.

Would it not be easier and safer simply to ask an appropriate committee of the university senate to review the university's compensation and outside employment policies with an eye to guarding more carefully those who might be given to abusing the faculty's traditional freedoms? But of course. And principles of management might suggest that you do just that. However, principles of leadership suggest otherwise.

Flee from regulations that may strengthen the weak but will surely weaken the strong.

CHAPTER EIGHT
SOME CALL IT PLAY
A CASE OF INTERCOLLEGIATE ATHLETICS

On any Saturday afternoon in an American fall, you can, by simply turning on your television set, watch a descendant of Louis XIV pace the sidelines as he directs, to the cheers of his subjects, the play of several dozen boys in a central courtyard. While no one holds the train of his silk cape off the ground, an attendant performs the technological age's version by following at a respectful distance and lifting the wires and cables that attach him to various telecommunication devices. But the lack of silk and ermine does not deceive you for one moment: Everyone in the bleachers that surround that court and everyone watching from reclining chairs in dens across the country knows who makes the sun rise.

This university football coach and the young who wear his colors constitute for many the focus if not the whole of their spiritual and cultural lives. Hence, when observers of *homo ludens* provide us with anecdotes of what might in a saner context serve as instances of advanced hysteria, we smile the indulgent and amused smile of recognition. For example, James Michener has recorded a clergyman's manner of coping with the soul-wrenching experience of being deprived of the University of Nebraska's home games as a result of having been transferred to a parish in Michigan. He built a shrine of Nebraska's great football players and on game days he sat there and meditated. Presumably, the way God intended. His Michigan parishioners were sympathetic, for, as Michener's informant said, " . . . they realize that religion requires a man to be faithful to what he believes" (*Sports in America*, Random House, New York, 1976, p. 219). And this bizarre theology is not limited to men. Michener goes on to describe a woman who expresses her creed in these words: "When we were first married my husband worked out a scheme by which we could each sell a pint of our blood and pick up enough money to see the Oklahoma-Texas game. He said that in a marriage it was important to get started right where fundamentals were concerned." Presumably, they lived happily ever after—providing the right team won.

When you link such forms of emotionalism to a belief that the Trojans' or the Terps' or the Cornhuskers' crossing into end zones is in some mystical fashion associated with manhood and Christian virtues that keep this country from falling prey to communist plots, you begin to understand the furor caused by the NCAA's periodic attempts since its inception in 1906 to curb the intercollegiate athletic system's excesses. You also gain some insight into the power of mice that roar. Few administrators now have the temerity to proclaim that "it can't happen here." They have watched too many of their colleagues field press conference questions related to drug abuse, point shaving, illegal recruiting, abuse of student athletes, and total disregard for academic standards not to experience some fear and trembling regarding the integrity of their own programs.

Even sports historians, not given to debating the appropriateness of a university as impresario, point to evidence that shows that schools since the Middle Ages have had to struggle to prevent sports from interfering with studies. No one has concluded that the struggle is over. It may be a rare administrator who will ever be asked to vote to abolish intercollegiate athletics on any American campus, or to turn the present teams to professional ones that are paid to carry the university's name to glory, or to ask universities to end their monopolistic training of professional players. However, it is an equally rare administrator in a rare university whose values regarding the place of sports in the baccalaureate experience are not tested by a booster club, an athletic director, a head coach, or a student athlete.

THE BACKGROUND

Your public comprehensive university (FTES 16,000) in the far western part of the country is pale and drawn from having lived so long in the shadow of the state's research university. Your students' combined SAT score of 920 is respectable, your faculty are dedicated and competent, your physical plant while aesthetically drab is serviceable. However, you are known as "Insurance University"; you accept 74% of those who apply; and the alumni of the state's research university's professional schools hold the best subscription seats in all theaters of power.

Three years ago, the university's newly appointed young, energetic, charismatic president diagnosed the pallor as symptomatic of an illness suffered by institutions that lacked recognition. Nothing fatal, nothing grave, nothing that a little place in the sun would not cure. Prescription: Football with a capital F. Move from Division II to Division I AA, double the size of the stadium, woo the alumni, flatter every automobile dealer and real-estate developer who will allow you to buy him a ticket to tailgating. Build a bonfire, cage the mascot, and buy pom poms—we're on a climb.

Initially, the faculty were stunned and a significant number were too winded with indignation to want to climb anything. The resulting debate was long and bitter and succeeded in dividing a once homogeneous faculty into two parties of roughly equal force. One group was excited by the prospective Saturday afternoon fever, while the other was nearly apoplectic at the thought of diverting funds and energies to such ends. The humanists had been particularly vocal in their opposition. Football players have since accused some of them, most frequently English professors, of harassment and unfair grading practices. The professors have lodged strong protests against the practice of coaches calling to introduce themselves and/or to check on the progress of their athletes.

Rumors of lowered admission standards for athletes, especially football players, lurk behind the doors of Old Main, and passion has rendered tailgating the equivalent of intellectual fraud.

THE HAPPENING

JUNE 15

The registrar posts a storm watch. Nothing terribly severe. There is no need to tape the windows and to roll up the awnings, but it could pick up strength given the campus's atmospheric pressure.

"Remember the running back Tom S. who did so well last year?"

"So well at what?"

"Running over the opposition, of course."

"Let me guess. He didn't do so well in his studies."

"Right. It's a complicated story, but it ends with his having been academically dismissed."

"For academic reasons, we dismiss over 500 students a semester. Some of these students are athletes. Why should this one trigger a storm?"

"Tom S. had earned the required GPA of 2.00, but this past spring term he failed the remedial writing course for the third time."

"I thought that you said that last year was his sophomore year. You mean to tell me that he was about to enter his junior year without having yet passed Remedial Writing? A student is required to pass that course with a "C" grade or better by the end of his first year."

"I know. You won't like this, but that's the complication. In this case an exception was made."

"Who made it and for what reason?"

"I'm tracking it down and I'll get back to you as soon as I have all the facts. I called because P.R. [assistant V.P. for academic services to whom the registrar reports] won't be back from the conference for a couple of days and Tom S.'s father has engaged a lawyer who just called to say that he was certain we could resolve the matter amicably."

JUNE 19
You receive from the registrar two letters without editorial comment.

January 2

Dear Assistant Vice-President P.R.

I started school two years ago. My football coach registered me. I didn't know what to take. Mostly general requirements. Then I was told I had to take a placement test. After that I had to take some developmantal courses. But I had passed all my courses the first semester with C. I didn't know I had a time limit to complete the writing course. So I took it the second semester of my Freshman year but only got an F. But because of the mix up my first semester (when I didn't know what to take) the Standards Committee let me try again this past semester. But again tough luck. After the first week I knew that this instructor hated football players (a woman). She sent me to a tutor. I tried but I got an F on the two big exams. So I decided to forget it and study in my other classes. She flunked me.

If you give me another chance and I get a different professor who doesn't hate athletes I know I can pass this course.

My attitude is much better. Please give me a brake.

Thank you

Tom S.

P.S. My coach is willing to tell you that I will work hard.

January 10

Dear Mr. S.

After reading your letter requesting exception to the time limit for completion of competency requirements in writing, and after our conversation, I have decided to grant your request. However, judging from your record, you have not had good advice on course selection and I urge you to take advantage of both the university's Academic Advising Center and Tutorial Services Center.

Your failure to receive a grade of "C" in Developmental Writing 100 this spring term will result in your loss of degree candidacy. There will be no further exceptions made in this regard.

With best wishes for a successful semester.

Sincerely,

P.R.
Assistant V.P. for
Academic Services

JUNE 22

You examine Tom S.'s transcript and there is no question that thus far he has majored in eligibility. The script is familiar:

Ceramics for Non-Art Majors
Physics for Poets

You and Your Health
Volleyball I
Basic Sign Language
Sex Education
Family Life
Bowling I
Review of Fundamentals of Mathematics
Developmental Reading

Add to the above a few introductory courses in history, sociology, and geography in which this student received a grade of "D" or "C" and you have the 2-year intellectual biography of someone whose eyesight has not been damaged by spending excessively long hours in the scriptorium.

JUNE 23
You meet with Assistant Vice-President P.R., a young, kind, hardworking, well-meaning man who has come up through the ranks of Student Services. Why had he granted Tom S. an exception to the time limit for completion of the competency requirement in writing? He can posit nothing but *ad misericordiam* arguments and he is appropriately contrite. Tom S. had been during his visit with P.R. quite distraught, as had his father during a telephone conversation intended as an honest plea for mercy. P.R. was reasonably certain that Tom S. had learned a valuable lesson and would henceforth take his studies more seriously. He was a clean-cut, polite, boy-next-door type who was naive enough not to have read the catalogue nor to have sought proper advising. His football coach and the athletic director had also called on his behalf. They think the world of Tom S. and of his family. In fact, Delegate C., who represents the family's county in the House, had also called a day or so after Tom S.'s letter of appeal had arrived just to inquire about the university's policies regarding developmental writing courses. He felt certain that in cases where a student had not been properly advised, the university would grant an exception.

JUNE 24—A.M.
Upon the advice of the chair of the Department of English, Professor T., the instructor who had failed Tom S. in his third attempt

to master Developmental Writing, calls you. Your last communication from Professor T. had been in the form of a turgid letter holding you personally responsible for the increase in bird droppings on her office window ledge due to the removal of an ornamental grate. She is angry, indignant, disgusted, and chagrined. Delegate C. representing a neighborhood county in the House had left a message for her to call him. She had found the message in her mailbox upon her return from a well-earned 3-week holiday in London. Since she is occasionally invited to speak to regional civic groups, she assumed that Delegate C. was about to extend just such an invitation. So you can well imagine her surprise when he began to question her reasons for having judged Tom S.'s writing deserving of an F. One forceful statement led to another. Finally, she had been obliged to tell him in no uncertain terms that she was not about to discuss a student's work with anyone but the student concerned or authorized university personnel, and, furthermore, that she wanted to know how his credentials allowed him to evaluate anyone's writing. She had read his letters to his "Dear Constituents" and had not been impressed. Whereupon, Professor T. had melodramatically dropped the receiver back in its cradle.

JUNE 24—P.M.
Delegate C. calls. He is angry, indignant, disgusted, and chagrined. He has every right to express concern about his constituents. Nobody, but nobody hangs up on him. You are distracted by subliminal images of pale green waves lapping a deserted golden beach.

JULY 10
Two letters arrive which you would like not to finish reading.

Letter #1 is signed by all the members of the Department of English. In essence, Professor T.'s colleagues support her without reservation. Such an unfortunate incident and similar ones which will undoubtedly follow had been foreseen and foretold. Consequently, they have prepared themselves to withstand pressures and are determined to hold on to their standards with a dead man's grip.

Letter #2 is signed by an attorney retained to defend the rights of Tom S.

Dear _____:

   We are requesting that Tom S. be permitted to attend ___
University next fall as a full-time student with all the rights and
privileges pertaining thereto. To that end we are requesting a
hearing with you so that you might have the benefits of the
facts and the law in this matter.
   We believe that the following will persuade you to rule in
the student's favor.

1. Tom S. scored 68 in a final examination when he apparently needed a score of 70 in order to pass a Developmental Writing course. Tom S. was denied the benefit
   of due process as outlined in the university's document,
   "Student Rights and Responsibilities" in that his final
   examination was never reviewed by other instructors in
   the department or by the chair of the department.

2. The week prior to the final examination, Tom S. was
   involved in an automobile accident as a result of which
   he suffered multiple injuries. These injuries caused him
   pain and headaches that made concentrated study impossible. While he was granted a 2-week delay before
   taking the examination, he did not fully recover for a
   month. A physician's report is attached.

3. Because Tom S. decided quite late in the summer preceding his freshman year to attend college at all, he did
   not take part in the regular summer orientation session
   offered all freshmen. The football coach and students
   associated with the football team, all of whom had
   worked hard to recruit Tom S., set up his schedule of
   courses. No one explained the time limit associated with
   the Developmental Writing course. That is the reason
   he never even attempted to register for it before the second semester of his freshman year. Then, he failed the
   course in this first attempt because he had to stop attending classes. He was literally exhausted at night from
   football practice and could not keep up with his work
   in this particular course.

4. Not only was Tom S. not properly advised regarding
   the time requirements for completion of Developmental
   Writing, but as the record shows, a university administrator has already waived a strict enforcement of the
   regulation by permitting Tom S. to register for the course
   a third time this past spring term.

5. Tom S. had neither received nor been asked to read the University catalogue.

This case concerns a student who was able to accumulate 56 credits with a 2.00 grade point average in a university that sets a time limit on the completion of a writing course on the grounds that students must have reached this level of proficiency before being adequately prepared to take university courses beyond freshman year. We request a complete hearing in order to present an oral argument that will show that Tom S. has not been treated fairly.

We believe that it is in the best interest of the university and of our client to reach an amicable resolution within the confines of the institution. However, should that prove infeasible, we are prepared to ask the court to grant an injunction that would allow Tom S. to continue his academic studies at _____ University with full rights and privileges pertaining thereto, pending a full hearing on the merits.

Very truly yours,

P. M. L.
Attorney at Law

Football practice begins August 1.

The reason P. M. L.'s name is familiar is that his brother is the vice-president of the Booster Club.

You call the university's attorney, a feminist whose initial response is that any male judge, who was not in youth snubbed by a cheerleader who preferred the charms of a football player to his own, will respond with sympathy to Tom S.'s plight.

SUGGESTED COURSE OF ACTION

You have suffered the indignity of being pushed into a pool fully dressed in your power-blue blazer. You can, of course, rise to the surface, but it is unlikely that you can climb out without some embarrassment. Dump the water out of your shoes and refuse to reinstate Tom S. as a full-time student.

Refuse also to meet with P. M. L., the student's attorney, but have the university's attorney respond to his letter. You should not fear a court's injunction because Tom S. has no contractual or constitutional right to continued enrollment. Injunctive relief rests on the discretion of a court and is an extraordinary remedy in cases that point to immediate substantial and irreparable injury. Once you have set aside whatever sympathy you may feel for the student, and whatever concerns may plague you regarding the assistant V.P.'s decision to grant an exception to a regulation that seems not only just but generous, and whatever anger you may need to control regarding the need for and abuse of developmental courses, what you are left with is quite simply the case of an academic dismissal for failure to fulfill a university's published requirements. Indeed, this student received two extensions of time within which to fulfill remedial coursework, and even then failed to meet the requirements. His predicament is one of his own making. Furthermore, there is no evidence that granting yet another exception would lead Tom S. to success. In educational law it is a given that courts in academic questions do not substitute their judgment for those made by faculty and administrators. In 1978, the Supreme Court in *Board of Curators of the University of Missouri* v. *Horowitz* (435 U.S. 78, 98 S.Ct. 948, 55 L. ED. 2d 124) made clear that a hearing was not required in academic dismissal cases.

You should certainly grant Tom S.'s request to have his final examination in Developmental Writing reviewed. Most departments have established written and detailed procedures to deal with such requests and these should now be followed to the letter of the law. Should the result of this review confirm Professor T.'s judgment, then Tom S. has been justly dismissed for academic reasons. Since the main purpose of establishing time limits for the successful completion of remedial courses is a university's interest in maintaining a respectable level of discourse in its classes, Tom S. could be allowed to repeat the course at issue until he runs out of patience and/or money providing he is not permitted to enroll in bona fide university courses. Since his grade point average is 2.00, he could petition a standards committee for readmission once and if he succeeds in slaying this dragon.

However, if an opera is not over until the fat lady sings, an academic case is not closed until the applicable policies and procedures have been questioned. In this instance, you have a great deal of work to do.

Request an invitation to meet with the faculty in the Department of English for the purpose of reaffirming common values and of reducing the level of anxiety which this incident has projected as upon a screen. Take care, however, not to give even the impression that you are to be considered a member of the underground. The president of the university has decided to place an emphasis on intercollegiate sports and you owe him loyalty. Your task is to maintain integrity in the academic under changed conditions.

Meet privately with Professor T. She should not be left with the fear, however, unacknowledged, that she behaved in an unacceptable fashion. No one is ever too old to need approval. While Miss Manners would not condone slamming telephone receivers down in the ears of anyone, including delegates from the House of Representatives, no professor should discuss the details of a student's performance with unauthorized outsiders.

Meet with P. R., the assistant V.P. for academic services, and point not only to the error of his ways but to the dangers of submitting to pressures from various constituents who are frequently at odds with one another. Tom S.'s request for a third attempt at Developmental Writing should have been forwarded to an academic standards committee that is or should be beyond the reach of soulful but unsubstantial appeals.

See that Tom S. is offered the services of the university's Academic Advising Center. If, indeed, his only academic advising came from coaches and fellow students, you have a hole in your net that should be mended immediately. Furthermore, how could one of your students have made so little progress in 2 years toward fulfilling either general university requirements or the requirements of a major in any discipline? The president of an institution fielding teams in Division I must according to the by-laws of the NCAA sign a certificate of compliance that guarantees among other things that "Each student–athlete who represents the institution in intercollegiate athletics competition during the academic year shall have been certified to be in good academic standing and maintaining satisfactory progress toward a degree . . ." Who would sign such a form for Tom S.?

Now, once you have trimmed all of these lower branches, find the courage to climb high enough to saw off that unsightly, dead limb. One of your students who has failed three times to pass a remedial writing course has managed with apparently unremarkable effort to accumulate 56 hours of credit with a cumulative GPA of 2.00.

Implications abound. Standards in classes have been lowered

to meet the abilities or preparation of those admitted. Papers are no longer assigned and essay examinations are no longer given in a great many lower division courses. The Physics is not for Poets but for players of video games. One does not need basic language skills in order to deal with abstract thought. One no longer deals with abstract thought. We have arrived at a nonliterate society where knowledge even in universities is not found primarily though not exclusively in books.

If you refuse to check any of the above, then you must undertake at least two projects:

1. On the grounds that writing is the only means of serious discourse, work with the chairs of departments and the university senate to establish a program of Writing Across the Curriculum. Literacy is not the exclusive responsibility of those who teach literary criticism.

2. Conduct a study of the transcripts of athletes, in accordance with the compliance regulations of the NCAA, to see how advisers have defined "satisfactory progress" in the freshman and sophomore years. Are athletes directed to register for certain courses? Certain sections of certain courses? How recently have standards committees and chairs of the departments that offer these courses reviewed the syllabi? What is the pattern of grading in these courses? Make it clear that there is no intent here of violating academic freedom or of impugning anyone's integrity. However, a university that does not care about its intellectual standards, is a university in name only.

To paraphrase Woody Allen, the stadium and the library might lie down together, but the library had better not sleep.

CHAPTER NINE
THE MISSING MICROSCOPES
A CASE OF INVENTORY CONTROL

Since we live in a culture weighed down by the things of this world, and since few persons outstride their age, one might have difficulty defending a position that claimed that a university's buildings radiate a spiritual aura greater than, say, the luggage department of a Neiman-Marcus. However, it is nevertheless true that a professor maintains his self-esteem by making points that add to knowledge, while an inventory clerk maintains his by doing counts that balance sheets. And to ask the first to enter the world of the second, or to expect the second to understand the values of the first is at times asking and expecting the impossible, but the necessary.

"In my day" stories from older colleagues who enjoy remembering a time when no one ever worried about expensive instruments disappearing from unlocked laboratory cabinets may be as charming and as touching as your grandmother's anecdotes about leaving the door of her cottage unlocked when she went as a young girl to her Tuesday quilting bee, but charm will no longer do. Modern colleges/universities are not retreat houses immune from contemporary problems associated with the seriously rising rates of theft. When churches open only at posted hours in an effort to guard gold ciboriums, few institutions are so geographically and culturally isolated as to afford the luxury of widely spaced inventories and lax security.

As a result, problems ranging from the proper role of armed guards in an institution of higher learning to shoplifting in campus bookstores abound. For an academic administrator, the most slippery of these problems often centers on a faculty's attitude regarding its responsibility in matters of inventory, particularly in departments, such as those in the sciences and fine arts, that require large amounts of expensive material and supplies for both research and teaching. A faculty member who will lock a Volkswagen Beetle to protect a salami sandwich and a thermos of coffee will leave a laboratory containing a half a million dollars worth of instruments unattended and unlocked while he spends 2 hours in discussion with a colleague in an office a half a block down the hall. Faculty who will howl in protest at the mere rumor of budgetary cutbacks for supplies will protest even more vociferously if asked to account for the 13 electronic balances, 4 film projectors, and 15 cameras that appear to have been mislaid.

THE BACKGROUND

The biology department within your university is of moderate size (38 full-time and 5 part-time faculty) and of regional reputation. While the faculty takes pride in its standards of excellence in teaching, 80% of them are convinced that such a level of teaching depends in important part on active scholarship. Consequently, those thus persuaded are actively engaged in ongoing research and field studies in nearby estuaries. Many maintain that for the greater portion of the year, they work a 60-hour week. When you add up research that is regularly published in professional journals and shared at conferences, a 12-hour teaching load, the advising of students, and a fair share of committee work, you have no trouble believing it.

Since morale in this biology department is high and you do not want to risk lowering it without grave cause, since these biologists do work as hard as they say they do, and since you have always avoided assigning all but the most necessary clerical tasks to professionals, you, much in the mode of your predecessor, have avoided giving thought to overhauling an inventory control system that you suspect would fail any sort of serious inspection. But, after all, you also are logging 60 hours and more a week. Surely, everyone knows that you just completed a restructuring of the Financial Aid Office, and that last year you rewrote the whole of the enrollment management plan. Besides, such an enterprise would involve another division, Business and Finance, and you know what these accounting types are like: They will surely accuse the faculty of negligence, and who knows where that will end. Anyway, it is not as if you had no system of inventory management at all. All purchased items are tagged and once a year the property control department mails its selective computer lists so that departmental secretaries and a departmental inventory clerk may match the tag numbers to the identification numbers on the computer printouts.

However, all of your rationalizing cannot defend you from

thoughts that pursue you like hooded phantoms in the night. Was that woman caught walking out of the biology building one evening last month with a microscope in the bottom of her shopping bag an example of what takes place often undetected? Are those many errors on the computer printouts truly, as the department chair who is about to retire claims, the result of clerical errors and careless bookkeeping in the department of property control? Is it true, as rumor has it, that inventory checks have not been taken seriously since the department grew to double its size a dozen years ago and that if a spot check reveals a missing item, it is "assumed" that "someone" has "borrowed" it?

THE HAPPENING

Chair A. of the biology department has retired and Chair B., his replacement, now has her own posters on the department's central office walls. Chair B., unlike former Chair A., is young, efficient, aggressive, and ambitious. In November of her first academic year in office, she informs you in writing that her predecessor had neglected his supervisory responsibilities in regard to the department's inventory clerk, and she hints that while every biologist was undoubtedly aware of this lapse in management, no one was eager for an improvement in accountability that would lead to tighter bureaucratic control. Both the tone of Chair B.'s memo and the accompanying copy of her letter to the clerk make it clear that she intends to indulge her prospensity for reform. The clerk, henceforth, is to arrive and leave his post on time, take but his allotted hour at lunch, and follow precisely the procedures printed in the property control manual. Any departure from such instructions will result in an evaluation rating considerably lower than the allegedly inflated ones that he has received in the past 3 years.

The clerk's reply, received within 4 days, rises like a white whale against the horizon. He is being harassed because last June he had written a memo, copy attached, to Chair A. indicating that 98 microscopes, including compound microscopes, dissecting microscopes, and illuminators, with a combined value of approximately $58,753.46 were missing from the department's inventory. He had never received a reply. Chair B.'s accusatory and insulting letter had persuaded him that he was being certainly threatened and possibly blackmailed. He had kept silent too long; his desire to give Chair B. time to settle in before reminding her of this major problem had been misguided; and if administrators did not take this matter of the missing instruments seriously, he would write the board of trustees, select members of the legislature, and, if necessary, the governor. Here was a man who had believed his football coach: a good defense was a strong offense.

Chair B.'s extensive search of former Chair A.'s files ferrets out nothing resembling a report of missing items from the clerk, but the biology department's secretary, who does recall seeing what is now referred to as "the June letter," discovers a box in the back of a stationery supplies storage closet containing what appears to be all the correspondence that had reached former Chair A.'s desk in the last 3 months of his tenure. Any problem that might have distracted from his daydreams of a planned departure for Tahiti, while not swept under the rug, had apparently been piled in the corner of a closet. As a conscientious child who can't get himself to throw away food will allow it to decay in the bottom of his knapsack, a conscientious man who no longer had the psychic energy to deal with complex issues, but who could not bring himself to destroy important correspondence, had sheltered it under temporary cover.

You write inventory clerk Y. to tell him that you have now received a copy of the June letter, that you are going to investigate the matter immediately, and that you will take appropriate action. The same day, you call the dean of the College of Arts and Sciences, who, of course, has been privy to all the details of the case and who has been copied on all correspondence, and you tell him that it is time to call a meeting of the biology department faculty for the express purpose of discussing the missing microscopes and inventory control. Since all regular meetings of this department are taped, this special session should be also.

Clerk Y.'s interpretation of "immediately" does not correspond to yours: 2 weeks after your memo to him and your call to the dean, you receive a copy of the clerk's letter to two members of the legislature who sit on the House Appropriations Committee. In it, he accuses the university's administrators of having done nothing about the missing microscopes since he brought the matter to their attention way back in June. Furthermore, as a consequence of his laudable undercover work, he is being harassed, his job is being threatened, and his car has been tampered with (tires were slashed and battery was stolen). The same mail brings a copy of a memo from Chair B. to her dean charging Clerk Y. with insubordination: he arrives late for work and has been conspicuously reading a bestseller entitled, *How to Uncover Fraud in Large Corporations,* while eating lunch in the department's faculty-staff lounge.

You call for an immediate delivery of the tape of the special meeting of the biology department, which took place yesterday, and by "immediate" you now mean "today." In summary, the tape reveals a not unusual faculty view: The problem, which they suspect has been grossly exaggerated though they admit they cannot account for the whereabouts of the instruments in question, belongs to property control clerks and not to research scientists. An immediate solution, however, would be to buy Clerk Y. a pair of cement shoes and to take him for a swim. You are not amused.

You meet with the dean and Chair B. The first opts for a thorough inventory of the department done by an outside firm, but the second, who is no longer certain that she wishes to go into administration, defends her faculty and accuses Clerk Y. of creating a diversion to draw attention away from his laziness and insubordination.

You are 4 months away from budget hearings before the House Appropriations Committee when part of the yearly ceremony includes genuflecting before the need, always loudly expressed, to protect the taxpayer's dollar.

SUGGESTED COURSE OF ACTION

Suspect no one; suspect everyone. Murders have been committed even in monasteries. Those in search of truth about the mating habits of hermit crabs are not thereby immune from temptation, and it would be naive to believe that professors who have been known to sell manuscripts stolen from libraries to pay mortgages are not imaginative enough to sell microscopes stolen from laboratories to support, say, a drug habit. In this case, your operative premise should be that anyone but the butler may have done it.

Hence, you must work energetically on two fronts. One, you must conduct an investigation that will reveal the exact nature and amount of the loss, the person(s) responsible for it, and policies and procedures that allowed it to occur. Two, you must inform, in writing, the president of your institution, who, I am assuming, has been aware of the unfolding of the tale. Then, you and/or the president should have lunch with the chair of the board of trustees and both (separately) House delegates from the ap-

propriations committee who received letters from Clerk Y. Call
for the luncheon appointments immediately, but schedule them
2 weeks hence so as to give you time to establish your plan of
action. Be prepared to present this plan in writing to each of your
luncheon guests. While all of these steps will cost you time, the
price you pay now will be but a fraction of the price you will be
charged later should anyone on or off campus decide to use this
episode for political gain.

The details of any plan of action will, in great part, be determined by the managerial structure of the university/college, but
the exclusion of any of the following items would very likely
weaken the possibility of closing this case without serious reper-
cussions and of persuading outside agencies that you are in control. And, however much you now wish you had followed Chair
A. to Tahiti, members of your board of trustees, delegates from
the House Appropriations Committee, and reporters, should the
press become interested, will all be watching and expecting de-
cisiveness. Therefore, your plan should include:

1. Hiring an outside firm to do a complete inventory of the Department of Biology and of any other department, such as
   physics or chemistry, housed in the same building. You should
   also at this time consider using bar codes on each item so that
   future inventories can be done using electronic scanners.
2. Transferring Clerk Y. from the Department of Biology to another department in another building until the results of the
   inventory are known. Whether to make the reassignment permanent should be the subject of review after the results of the
   inventory are known.
3. Establishing a committee, chaired by the dean, of senior faculty
   members from all departments in this science building, upper
   classmen majoring in one of the disciplines in question, and
   personnel from the central offices of property control and campus-wide security for the purpose of examining present policies
   and procedures governing inventory and security and of making recommendations for improvement. The examination might
   include consultation with state legislative auditors if appropriate.
4. Filing a report with the campus security about suspected thefts
   in the building in question and asking for a confidential memo
   outlining their planned investigation.

You should bring the full weight of your office to bear upon the need to receive the inventory report and the committee recommendations at least 2 weeks before you have to appear before the House Appropriations Committee, and you should once more discuss *viva voce* the results of both with the chair of the board d and the two House delegates who have been involved from the beginning. You should by now have these two delegates running interference for you.

Finally, during these months you and the dean of Arts and Sciences should have been meeting with the faculty involved to persuade them of the seriousness of the case and to explain their role in inventory control. Be prepared to hear that a complete inventory had been taken one summer 10 years ago by athletes who could not read; that incompetent clerks tag everything including the faculty's personal property; that students tear off property control tags; that the inadequate budget you give them forces them to cannibalize instruments; that shipments of instruments are misdirected after tagging; that the dollar value of certain instruments is pulled from imaginary catalogues; that the housekeeping staff leaves doors unlocked; that faculty and students should have access to the building 24 hours a day, for research, unlike administration, is not done on a 9 to 5 schedule. All of the above may approach truth to varying degrees; none of the above completely absolves faculty, staff, and students from responsibility.

Never let sleeping dogs lie if upon waking they might unexpectedly attack you.

CHAPTER TEN
UN WHOPPER AVEC FROMAGE, PLEASE
A CASE OF PROGRAMS ABROAD

Travel is in the air. Members of the Senate and of Congress suffer the amenities of the Beirut Hilton in search of diversion disguised as information. Cultural exchanges flourish: Argentineans dance the tango in New York; Indians play the sitar in San Francisco; Americans hang in Geneva paintings conceived in Santa Fe. Mayors and 30-member delegations adopt sister cities, exchange football jerseys for Mao Tse-Tung workers' frocks, and praise novelty under the illusion of praising culture. Businessmen/women study Japanese and Chinese in hopes of influencing the Oriental mind in its purchase of microchips. International business is the chic undergraduate discipline.

Never mind that the Guangzhou (formerly Canton) hotel's coffee shop reportedly employs waitresses whose name tags identify them as "Kitty" and "Polly," and that only a romantic literary pilgrim could discern a shade of difference between a rum and coke in Harry's Bar in Venice and a rum and coke in Hank's Tavern in Kansas City. Le Paris Drugstore plays "Purple Rain"; the Montparnasse train station sells "tickets" instead of "billets"; the French students at the Sorbonne wear Boston University warm-ups; and the American I. M. Pei has dug a huge hole in the center courtyard of the Louvre. Edith Piaf is dead, but we still yearn for the authentic foreign experience.

From the days of the postbaccalaureate grand tour of La Belle Epoque, to those of expatriation in the name of art between the two world wars, to the establishment of junior years abroad, to concentrated mini-mester quality time experiences in foreign lands, American professors and their students have bought backpacks and Wallabys and queued at shipping piers and airline terminals in the touching hope, to use Jamesian terms, of seeing "everything."

The rarely questioned faith in the educational benefits of travel abroad may spring, at least in part, from values that most academicians and their students are willing to accept as givens: that viewing phenomena from a foreign perspective without intermediary will add depth and scope to one's own provincial insights; that Americans raised on a diet of comparatively young culture need the invigorating supplement of the traditions of the past from which theirs sprang; and, finally, that there are ways of apprehending truth that transcend the systematic and traditional ones associated with the average classroom.

Now, precisely how an attempt to see the Jamesian "everything" by wending a path through the crowds of the Kasbah in Algiers or by standing before Michelangelo's house of birth in Florence relates to an institution's mission is a complex question not always answered satisfactorily and, indeed, at times not even asked.

THE BACKGROUND

Your small women's college (FTES 950) is located in one of the Southern states. It is well endowed, respectful of traditions, and attached to such anachronistic rituals as Father/Daughter dances in May and dressing every evening for dinner. Your recruitment efforts succeed in attracting primarily young women of the upper middle class who are refused admission at Wellesley and Smith or who are unsympathetic to the New England's schools' reputation for strenuous cerebral gymnastics. Nearly everyone plays tennis, drives a car received as a high school graduation gift, and feeds Izod's alligator. Not a few of the alumni are the mothers, aunts, and grandmothers of the present undergraduates. On Saturday afternoons one rides horses owned by the college on bridle paths meticulously maintained by the grounds crew or one takes hours preening for a date while lolling on beds covered by darling "Gotta Getta Gund" bears. During the week, one works toward attaining the female version of a gentleman's Cs.

The faculty, considering intense scholarship as vulgarly competitive, avoid national professional meetings, preferring small gatherings of their own kind for the exchange of views. They are, however, cultured, urbane, and, according to some, excruciatingly well mannered. Unfortunately, according to others, in this homogeneous world have entered in the past dozen years or so Berkeley and New York University types whose world view is not entirely congenial. While these aliens had originally been offered appointments because the college's tenured faculty found it increasingly difficult to locate sympathetic native sons and because the administration was blind to the benefits of cloning, the aliens themselves had accepted the appointments in a foreign cultural setting *faute de mieux:* The call for Ph.D.s, especially in the humanities, had become nearly inaudible. Once aboard, however, the latter had found both the ship's pace and the ship's amenities far more pleasing than they had anticipated. Furthermore, they soon discovered both a pleasure and a cause in scandalizing the bourgeois world with perspectives imported not only from California and New York but from South Africa and Poland and Israel.

During the same dozen years or so, your administrative team has without fanfare but with determination raised academic standards, recruited with generous scholarships many who could not unaided have afforded the college's tuition, and dispelled some of the claustrophobic atmosphere both in the classroom and in the student-life activities. Consequently, a significant and growing minority of students, referred to in the vernacular of an earlier era as "eggheads"—even slang turned over slowly in this climate—are now taking the life of the mind seriously and are even in a defiant gesture of eccentricity choosing careers and letting marriage fall where and when it may.

As part of this subdued undermining of provincialism, the college has instituted a 3-week 3 credit-bearing mini-mester course called, "The Great Cities of the World." The plan is to change the "Great City" year after year. Paris has been chosen as the inaugural site. The hope is to provide an international experience for those students who cannot afford or do not wish to spend junior year abroad. Presumably the rich would profit from a short stay in a major foreign city that included far more than shopping at Galeries Lafayette or eating a Poire Belle Hélène at the Café de la Paix, and the less well off would be given an opportunity through competitive awards to study abroad.

THE HAPPENING

Only two members of the faculty, both historians, had volunteered to guide the first mini-mester adventure on French soil, but the competition for the post was not diminished by the paucity of candidates. Indeed, if anything it had been increased, for the two so engaged had been locked in cold war for several years. Professor B., a highly cultured middle-aged man sporting impeccable though ice-stiff manners and favoring ironic stances and language was respected, admired, and disliked by virtually all of his colleagues and feared by many of his students. A man of modest means, he viewed the teaching of this course as an opportunity to earn 3 weeks in a well-loved city. His knowledge of French was at best serviceable. Professor C., an equally cultured younger man, wore his learning far more lightly and was given to manners that were both casual and distracted. He was somewhat careless in dress and behavior and inspired the same amused goodwill that one willingly gives a St. Bernard. He was not above teasing Professor B. for his manicured life, and the latter, who took himself very seriously, had welcomed every opportunity to attempt to thwart the younger man's initial appointment and subsequent advancement. In this instance, he writes you a long letter in Victorian prose explaining why Professor C. was unsuited for this post.

The chair of the Department of History, the director of the Junior Year Abroad Program, and the chair of the Curriculum Committee had all recommended that the assignment be given to Professor C. and you had seen no serious reason to substitute your judgment for theirs. Your one faint reservation, often expressed by others *sotto voce*, was that Professor C., whose wealthy parents had left him without the protection of the need to work, occasionally indulged his penchant for harmless but unrestrained behavior. This salient characteristic often manifested itself in what the British novelist Elizabeth Taylor once described as having "inconvenient plans for other people's pleasure." In the most good-natured manner he insisted on feeding you when you were determined to lose weight; on buying another round when you should have arrived home an hour ago; on providing you with the latest work of an author who interested you not at all.

Professor C. spoke French fluently and had made frequent cross-Atlantic journeys. A by-product of such adventures had been post cards mailed to his students and then tacked to residence halls bulletin boards. They were renowned for their sophomoric innocent humor and quoted widely: "Greetings from Firenze. While touring a spaghetti factory near Florence yesterday, a tourist fell into a vat of tomato sauce and became a seasoned traveler. Wish you were here." The recipients of such cards were evenly divided between those who could not understand why Professor C. had never married and those who could.

SATURDAY, DECEMBER 28

Professor C., accompanied by 10 persons who have registered for the course, "Great Cities of the World: Paris," boards a plane for Charles De Gaulle Airport. Once there, he and his fellow pilgrims are to lean their staves in a small hotel within walking distance of the Sorbonne and the Musée de Cluny. The group, in addition to Professor C. and six of the college's regular undergraduates, includes two male seniors from a nearby public university and two middle-aged women who have returned to college for a second baccalaureate degree in an attempt to dust and polish careers shelved 20 years ago.

MONDAY, JANUARY 20

As you look out from your office window at the flowering camellia shrubs and still feel with enjoyment the weight of your old ski boots worn just yesterday for one last run on the slopes of the Green Mountains of Vermont, the phone rings. Mrs. G., the well-known voluble mother of a timid and shy undergraduate who was one of the 10 registrants for the mini-mester course in Paris, wishes to speak to you.

> "Good afternoon, Mrs. G. How are you? Well, I hope." "Honestly. I'm surprised you dare ask how I am." "Why? What's the trouble?" "The trouble is—and you should know—that I can't remember when I've been so angry. Last night I drove to the airport to pick up my daughter and learned for the first time that Professor C. had not returned with the students. Did you know that?" "No, I did not." "And did you know that the students had been left to fend for themselves before boarding the return flight at De Gaulle and then in transferring from Kennedy to La Guardia in New York? I can't speak for the other students, but I can assure you that Caroline experienced severe anxiety as a result of this irresponsible act. And that's not all. It took me half the night, but I got a full account of this so-called study trip, and the details are not such that I want to describe them over the phone. Caroline and I would like to see you this afternoon. I want you to hear this very sorry tale from her."

As you wonder if the Vermont ski patrol hires persons over 40, you set an appointment with Mrs. G. and her daughter, Caroline, who is unlikely to do the telling.

Mrs. G., a woman of presence and a born Southern storyteller luxuriates in details that frame both characters and events as Caroline, eyes downcast, sits uncomfortably poised for flight. Once the quiver is emptied, you are left with the following wounded. On the day of the scheduled return flight, Professor C. and Mrs. K., a widow and one of the two older women who had registered for the course, had chosen to extend their experience abroad by flying to Geneva instead of New York. Since classes are to resume on February 3, Professor C. had undoubtedly reasoned that he was free to take a short holiday. The offense, if it be one, could have come as no surprise to those unfortunate enough to have witnessed their dalliance throughout the past 3 weeks in Paris. In a shameless, flaunting manner, Professor C., encouraged by Mrs. K., had behaved as a boulevardier pursuing a cocotte. Mrs. G. had read her Proust. Indeed, he had been so single-minded at this task that all other obligations had been neglected. Here was an outline of what had passed for a syllabus, and others are prepared to support Caroline's contention that the few items checked had been the only promises kept. When prodded, Caroline, clearly in misery, nodded that such was the case. Evening after evening the students had been left to their own devices. Before leaving the States, Professor C. had asked the students to keep a diary of their observations and insights while in Paris. Mrs. G. wishes you to read Caroline's. The only possible conclusion to be drawn from such a reading, as you will discover, is that the students would have learned as much had they spent 3 weeks in Paris, Texas.

No one opens a diary, even one intended for public scrutiny, without experiencing the slight chill of peeking through the keyhole of someone else's soul. In this case, to the chill is added the pathos of reading in a child's hand such quivering anorexic thoughts on such rich vellum bound in genuine leather.
Sample relevant entries:

> Wednesday, January 1. Professor C. had us get up real early because he wanted us to go to a Catholic Church miles away and attend a service. We took a subway to a place called Pigalle and climbed this huge hill like those in San Francisco to reach this real ugly church called Sacré Coeur. I was never so cold in my life. But on our way back we saw the outside of the Moulin

Rauge (SP.?) and that was fun because we have pictures of it on coasters at home. After that, Professor C. said that since this was a holiday we could have the day to do anything we wanted. Professor C. went someplace with Mrs. K. and the others went someplace too, but Isabelle and I couldn't think of where to go and it was so cold that we stayed in our room and played cards. I wish Mother was here because she can always think of something to do. I miss her.

Monday, January 6. Another boring day. They call it the Feast of Kings and it's a mini holiday. Even Professor C. couldn't think of anything for all of us to do together so he and Mrs. K. left after lunch to visit a friend of Professor C. who lives in Paris. Whenever I try to speak French, the French speak English. I wish now that I had signed up for Spanish instead of French.

Thursday, January 9. This morning we took the Metro (that's what they call subways here) and went to a cemetery like you've never seen before. It's called Father La Chaise cemetery and lots of famous people are buried here. Like Chopin and Sarah Bernhart. Professor C. showed us all around and told us the story of how during the French Revolution they fought among the graves. That was neat. Greg and Mike from the State University are real impolite to Professor C. sometimes. Isabelle says that it's because Professor C. doesn't do all the things the list said we would do. I don't mind because museums can be pretty boring and besides it's not his fault if he doesn't always meet us because the Paris Metro is always breaking down and there are lots of traffic jams. The same thing happens to Mrs. K. After all, this isn't America. Professor C. is always nice to me. He's friendly to everybody and he's always in a good mood.

Tuesday, January 14. This morning we visited a church called St. Roch and saw some more tombs. I'm getting a little sick of churches. So I was glad when Professor C. said that instead of following the list this afternoon, we could do whatever we wanted. Greg and Mike got real mad and they argued with Mrs. K. and Professor C. Isabelle and I went to see "The Flick of Beverly Hills" and had a real good time. It was neat to see the French subtitles. Tomorrow we go visit Napoleon's tomb. I'm getting a little sick of tombs too.

With ease, you could forecast that letters calling for an *auto-da-fe* would arrive within a few days. The first came from the second of the two older women who registered for the course.

January 22

I believe that if you investigate Professor C.'s mini-mester travel/study course conducted in Paris which ended just a few days ago, you will discover that he used it to further his own personal interests rather than those of the group to whom and for whom he was responsible.

Professor C. conducted an open flirtation with one of the students throughout our stay in Paris and spent the entire time tending to her needs while ignoring those of the other students. I personally got to the point where I felt I was intruding on their time together when I went anywhere under the guidance of Professor C.

In addition to the unprofessional conduct referred to above, I feel that the course was misrepresented in that many events (lectures, plays, museum visits) listed in the original description of the course never materialized. I'm tempted to ask for a refund.

The final insult came on the last day of the course when Professor C. announced that he and Mrs. K. (his girlfriend) would not be returning to New York with us because they had decided to spend a week in Geneva. Consequently, we were expected to make our own way through the maze of airports when this had been described as a fully escorted travel/study course. Fortunately, the two young men from the State University knew enough French to get us through Charles De Gaulle airport.

I would hate to see the high standards of our college marred by one irresponsible, indifferent man. I urge you to take proper action.

Sincerely,

———

On the heels of this letter, you receive one from the two male State University students. Their indignation springs from a somewhat different source.

January 23

You will by now have received several complaints from students who took your college's travel/study course in Paris this mini-mester. Some will probably have objected to Professor C.'s carrying on with one of the older students and his having "abandoned" us in what is probably the most civilized city in the world. Frankly, we couldn't care less. Professor C. can romance a stone as far as we're concerned, and we certainly weren't in need of a baby-sitter. We were, however, in need of a teacher. Otherwise, we would have gone to Paris on our own.

This so-called course was to a genuine academic experience what sandlot ball is to professional baseball. Professor C. behaved as if he had never seen his syllabus and shared information which we could have gotten from a Michelin Guide. He spent 3 weeks pursuing his own whims and invited us to join him whenever his moods allowed. In sum, the experience turned out to be a do-it-yourself project bearing a custom-made price tag.

This was our third travel/study abroad course so we did have something to compare this one with. Last winter we signed up for a London Theater course and the winter before that we went to mainland Ecuador to study the biological relationships of the Andean highlands and tropical rainforests. Both of these courses were sponsored by our own university and were absolutely terrific.

If private schools run their shop this loosely, we're certainly happy that we chose to go to a public one.

Sincerely,

Gregory L.
Michael L.

P.S. We're sending you a copy of our journals of this trip so you can read and weep.

TUESDAY, JANUARY 28

You read the young men's journals. While you do not weep, you do cringe here and there at the Viking Line tour description of the adventure.

You meet with the chair of the history department and the chair of the College Curriculum Committee. The first admits that Professor C. may have been guilty of indiscretion and a certain degree of laissez-faire, but he is certainly not prepared to believe every letter he reads and implies that neither should you. The second, concedes that questions had been raised by members of the Curriculum Committee regarding what appeared to have been a somewhat disjointed syllabus, but the proposal and supporting material had been submitted late, Professor C. had been pressured to meet certain printing deadlines for advertisements of the course, and most had agreed to view the first such mini-mester course as a shakedown cruise. Professor C., after all, was an intelligent, knowledgeable man who knew France well and students were bound to profit from a trip to Paris under his guidance. All three of you agree that, of course, the concert should not end until Professor C. has been given his opportunity to conduct the score. He is scheduled to return from Geneva on Saturday, February 1.

TUESDAY A.M., FEBRUARY 4
You receive an elegantly simple note from Professor B.

February 3

Je vous l'avais dit.

Sincerely,

Professor B.

He had, indeed told you and everyone else so.

TUESDAY P.M., FEBRUARY 4
You meet with Professor C., who is winded but cheerful and un-buttoned. Look, so he flirted with a middle-aged woman who flirted back. It seems to him inappropriate to behave as if he had been caught *in flagrante delicto* in one of the restrooms of Pan Am flight 402. He denies neglecting the students. He had not followed a rigid schedule because it seemed stupid to do so. He had gone with the flow. Listen, he had even taken the students to the Sacré Coeur one morning when it was so frigid he knew he would catch a cold. He wanted them to have the experience. They got back all right did they not? He had hardly deserted a group of Girl Scouts with bags of cookies at De Gaulle. In that group was a woman all too clearly on the wrong side of 40 and two male uni-

versity students who were experienced travelers. Of course, he expected the students to do background readings to prepare themselves for what they saw and he told them to keep a journal, which he has every intention of reading and grading. All right, not every single expectation was spelled out in the syllabus, but he had had little time to plan. Besides, he is opposed to unnecessary rigidity. Come on, place all of this in context. He preferred Mrs. K. to another woman of appropriate age who is so lonely she flirts with waiters; he ignored the surliness of two university self-conscious intellectuals who are possibly gay; he refused to hold the hand of a pathologically timid and insecure young undergraduate whose domineering mother keeps her on the verge of hysteria. And you are prepared to take the complaints of these people seriously? He will grant you this: he is not cut out to be a cicerone. You have his word that he will never teach a travel/study course again. So you need not worry.

MONDAY, FEBRUARY 10

Two of your undergraduates who had taken the trip and from whom you had not yet heard write to assure you that the mean things being said about Professor C. were just not true. He is a wonderful man and they loved the course.

SUGGESTED COURSE OF ACTION

Deny Professor C. a merit pay increase for a period of 2 years and deny him, in addition, permission to conduct a travel/study course for a period of 5 years. While he claims that he will never again seek such an assignment, the promise is made under emotional duress in that he finds it necessary at the moment both to appease and to reassure you. Remember your Jane Austen: "Their intended excursion to Whitwell turned out very differently from what Elinor had expected. She was prepared to be wet through, fatigued, and frightened; but the event was still more unfortunate, for they did not go at all" [from *Sense and Sensibility*].

Professor C. is guilty of unprofessional conduct on three counts.

1. He had led the students to believe that he would act as guide throughout the duration of the course, and, while his time sheet would be filled out differently by different

students, he obviously did not follow the syllabus, however disjointed, that had formed the basis of expectations for most registrants. Furthermore, he had not fulfilled his obligation to oversee the return portion of the journey.

2. He conducted an amorous liaison with one of the students to the certain distraction and probable neglect of the rest of the class. The student's age has no bearing on the case. The relationship between Professor C. and Mrs. K. was that of teacher and pupil and Professor C. was responsible for assigning her a grade in the course. He has exercised the power of his position in a totally inappropriate manner. The college has a right not to fear that its faculty will behave as innocents abroad. The naivete and prejudice of extending Cervantes's "When thou art at Rome, do as they do at Rome" to cover tacky manners judged as unacceptable in Charleston or Savannah are not qualities of mind that any academic institution need tolerate in those who teach its travel/study courses.

3. Based upon the testimony of the two male university students and that of the second older student, and based upon a reading of several of the diaries, and based upon the admission of the chair of the Curriculum Committee, you can reliably conclude that the course lacked intellectual rigor and that the academic credits given for its successful completion were highly inflationary.

Unfortunately, no one had heeded the evidence that neither Professor B. nor Professor C. were suited for this special assignment. Equally unfortunate is that those responsible for the approval of the whole admit that the course had been conceived and planned under the pressure of deadlines, ironically self-imposed, and that reservations had been dismissed for the sake of meeting them.

Maintaining the academic integrity of programs abroad whether they be conducted as year-long courses of study at centers owned and operated by colleges/universities or structured as 3-week backpack adventures requires eternal vigilance and unswerving convictions. A lecture before a Watteau in the Louvre should not be canceled for *soldes* at Printemps any more than a lecture on Winslow Homer at the National Gallery is postponed for a sale at Neiman-Marcus.

Every academic institution that establishes a course of study

abroad should first establish policies that will govern such programs and then adhere to these policies conscientiously. Regional
accrediting associations and the National Education Association's
Division of Education Travel have drafted guidelines for study
abroad and all insist upon clearly defined objectives, agreed upon
language proficiency requirements, extensive orientation sessions,
specific and honest descriptions of opportunities, a carefully selected director, criteria for judging performance that accord with
the standards of the home institution, and periodic review and
evaluation of the enterprise. In this case, the college has been
remiss on nearly every count.

Why all the structuring? Would not students learn by the very
act of leaving Ames and Portland and Los Angeles and spending
even a short period of time in Paris or Florence or Moscow? Of
course they would learn something, but not the systematized
"something" for which colleges/universities give academic credits.
To look at the spire of the Sainte-Chapelle is one thing; to see and
to give evidence of having seen the spire of the Sainte-Chapelle
is another. Having said that, however, one should immediately
remember that not all effective and lasting ways of learning are
limited to the formal and traditional classroom. It is important to
be told or to read that the sitar was invented in the thirteenth
century, that it has 7 main strings that play melody and 13 strings
that resonate underneath. It is equally important to hear someone
play it in West Punjab while surrounded by the sights and smells
and sounds of an Indic culture.

A solitary foreign travel that feeds both the mind and heart
requires effort, preparation, and wisdom. Structuring for others
a travel/study program that will do more than share sights that
satisfy a poster-dream vision of life demands no less. But the rewards are impressive. While the contemporary student may leave
an American airport without the knapsack, dagger, and staff of
the young seventeenth- and eighteenth-century European artisan
embarking on his wanderyear, he often does clutch the same hope
of gaining mastery. Rarely are American students who have been
properly oriented more eager to learn, more open to the best in
foreign cultures, more free of prejudices than they are when traveling abroad. And they truly do see: both through windows and
into mirrors.

The novelist, David Plante, has given a moving account of
his first trip to Paris (*New Yorker*, June 4, 1984) taken in 1959 when
he was 19. Of his first night there, he writes: "I lay on my back

in the middle of the hard, sagging bed, my chin on my chest because of the bolster under my head. I did not think: How uncomfortable this is. I thought: This is how Europeans sleep." Plante did not sleep that night, but neither did he sleep the next day, nor the day after that. And is not the purpose of all our efforts to avoid sleep?

Do not run with a travel/study program abroad before you have caught it.

CHAPTER ELEVEN
THE SKILLS OF INSPECTOR MAIGRET
A CASE OF FACULTY MISCONDUCT

I once listened to a young instructor complain about having prepared a party to which no one had come. He was a bright, knowledgeable, genuinely friendly young man given to the cultivation of a highly informal personal appearance that matched a deliberate and effective, equally informal, style of teaching. The Fu Man Chu moustache, the western boots, the open-necked flannel shirt were all part of a self-consciously relaxed mode of dress that was in keeping with his conducting discussion groups while sitting in a lotus position on top of his classroom desk. In the second month of his first year of teaching in a large-size public university, he had quite casually invited a freshman class of students, who had been encouraged to call him by his first name, to drop by his apartment near the university on a Sunday morning for coffee and doughnuts. No one had come. He was hurt, embarrassed, and, above all, puzzled. His colleagues, while sympathetic to varying degrees, were of little help: The neophytes were equally puzzled and the veterans were amused and/or patronizing.

Any number of widely varied styles may lead to success in teaching providing an individual's modus operandi is a genuine reflection of his personality and not an artificial adoption of manners that properly belong to someone else. And no doubt an instructor's style as a professional will determine many aspects of his relationship with students ranging from having or not having a beer with them in the university's Union to inviting them to his home. However, regardless of style, the propriety and wisdom and, in some cases, the ethics of certain patterns of behavior between a faculty member and his students must always take into consideration a campus's culture and the professional standards of conduct that by consensus apply in all instances.

Our party-giving, mustachioed friend, for example, had as an undergraduate attended a small, exclusive, private, New England college where wealthy, sophisticated students were very much at ease in professors' homes, and he had attempted to transfer a custom from this culture into the quite foreign land of an urban state institution whose students were the, often intellectually intimidated, sons and daughters of immigrants and minorities. One aspect of style, in this case, clearly called for study and modification. On the other hand, sexual harassment of students, for instance, is inappropriate, unwise, and unethical in colleges/universities of any size, characteristics, or culture.

THE BACKGROUND

Your regional university contains a School of Business and Economics that deserves its reputation as the academically weakest of the institution's 10 colleges/schools. For a dozen years before your arrival, it had been allowed to grow without benefit of either serious long-range or strategic planning, been allowed to drift under a very weak dean who had provided no leadership and barely adequate management, and been allowed simply to respond to the immediate needs and pressures of a local high-technology industry interested in students prepared only for entry-level positions. A flagship institution some 30 miles away has had its School of Business accredited and enjoys a prestige to which your competitors are inclined to refer in your presence.

The difficulties you must overcome in order to bring about improvement are the traditional ones: A significant number of undistinguished faculty whose willingness to teach large classes had been rewarded with tenure; a role as understudy assigned to you by both promising faculty and students who view the flagship university as the diva; a maddeningly slow progress in persuading regional CEOs to support your efforts to achieve quality; and a faculty housed in the university's other colleges/schools who resent the School of Business and Economics's mediocrity, and who view its faculty, with the exception of the economists, as non-academicians whose intellectual concerns, if, indeed, they have any, as beneath notice.

To make matters worse, a sizable group of the older, tenured faculty in this school, again with the exception of the economists, who yearn to be transferred en masse to the College of Liberal Arts, have formed a cabal that resents your calling for higher standards of professionalism, and that snipes at you from every bush on campus. Many of those not hidden in bushes are busy acting as consultants.

Understandably, you and a dean who was appointed a year and a half ago have spent little time wondering whether such a faculty inappropriately and unwisely dines with its marketing majors.

THE HAPPENING

Three weeks into the spring semester, young, untenured Assistant Professor W. in the School of Business and Economics's Department of Accounting (FTE faculty 26) has obtained permission from his department chair to bring a dozen of his most interested students to New York City for the weekend to attend a series of lectures sponsored by one of the largest accounting firms in the country. Three other newly appointed young instructors have also registered for the series of lectures, and all have reserved rooms in a midtown hotel in which the conference is to take place.

The week following the event, you receive a copy of an anonymous letter, mailed to the chair of the accounting department and to the dean of the school, in which the writer accuses Professor W., who was to act as the students' guide, of having behaved on the New York trip in an "outrageous fashion." In a word, he had gone out drinking with the students, had been overheard regaling them with stories about the ineptitude of his senior colleagues, and had held a party in his room that would undoubtedly have gone on all night had not the writer called the management to put a stop to it at 3:00 a.m.

While you are not in the habit of taking action urged upon you by anonymous letters, in this instance, both you and the dean agree that the chair of the department should have a talk with Professor W., not for the purpose of confirming the allegations, but in hopes of offering a junior faculty member possibly needed counsel. A short while after the chair's meeting with Professor W., which reportedly had gone well, the latter requests a repeated visit in order to express concern about one of his colleagues, who, not incidentally as you immediately suspect, had also attended these New York seminars. Apparently, she also had taken a bite of the Big Apple.

Professor W. had, in the last week, received two signed letters, one from a student and one from an alumnus, who, in effect, accused Professor Y., a second year instructor, of having made clear that her judgment of the quality of their work in a directed reading course would be colored by the quality of their work, in case one, in babysitting assignments and, in case two, in odd jobs done in and about her home. Bonnie A. claimed that she had not been paid for her babysitting work because, as Professor Y.'s friend, it had been understood that in return she need not worry about her final grade in her course. Professor Y. had been sympathetic to the notion that concentrating on course work was nearly impossible when you had just broken up with your boyfriend. After all, students had other lives to live. However, she had recently been confiding in Professor W., who had explained the error of her ways. Besides, she had since made up with her boyfriend, was no longer free to babysit, and Professor Y. was now applying pressure on her to hand in overdue papers. Clyde B.'s letter was far less whiny and far more aggressive: He had recently dropped by his old fraternity house and had overheard a male student, not a fraternity brother, but a visitor, brag about this semester being party time. This young chick in accounting had practically guaranteed him an ace in a tough directed reading course if he did work for her around the house and ran her errands. Now, there was a prof who was friend . . . lee. Clyde B. had had to work for his degree, and he was appalled by the unethical behavior of Professor Y. He would certainly never encourage anyone to attend his alma mater if his former instructor, Professor W., were unable to persuade the administration to discipline Professor Y.

Professor Y. vehemently denies all accusations of wrongdoing. While, admittedly, she had hired Bonnie A. to babysit and the second student to do odd jobs, she had paid both of them in cash for these services. She cannot imagine what reasons they might have for wanting to damage her reputation, but she has no such difficulty understanding Professor W.'s motives. Not only has he been driven by professional jealousy ever since the publication of her last major paper, and not only has he treated her as his rival since she first joined the department, but someone had told him that she was the one who had written and complained about his behavior with students on the New York trip. In addition, everyone knows him to be a male chauvinist. Her only mistake had been to send that letter anonymously. She plans to hire a lawyer and she advises Professor W. and both accusing students to do the same. Her threats have apparently frightened all concerned into doing just that, for in no time you begin to receive letters that begin, "My client . . ." In addition, the chair of the department and the dean of the school report repeated telephone calls from the parents of both students involved. They have taken a firm stand: Their children have been led into temptation, and Professor Y.'s head should be brought in upon a platter.

SUGGESTED COURSE OF ACTION

While as an administrator you are expected to be attuned to the vagaries of human nature, you should take care not to allow anyone to inveigle you into playing the role of Inspector Maigret. A surface and initial consideration of this case could easily entice the amateur detective in anyone to attempt to discover "who done it." Was Professor W. seeking revenge for Professor Y.'s having written that anonymous letter? Had Professor W. sought out and urged Bonnie A. and the alumnus to make these accusations? What was his own relationship with this student and former student? What did the student and former student expect to gain, if anything? What had caused the bad blood between Professors W. and Y. in the first place? Was it simply a matter of spontaneous combustion? And, above all, had Professor Y., indeed and in effect, agreed to sell grades? And, if so, what had led a bright young woman to risk her career for such small stakes? All intriguing questions that could preoccupy you and distract you from a far more central issue: the unprofessional climate in which such behavior grew. Let others wash the wings of seagulls earthbound by an oil slick; your obligation is to seek and to eradicate the cause of the spill.

The pedestrian actions to be taken amount to asking the university's attorney to communicate with the "clients'" attorney; to state unambiguously the precise code of professional conduct Professor Y. is charged with having broken; to set in motion the appropriate review committees or authorities on campus to conduct an inquiry; to inform everyone that, in fact, such an inquiry is in progress and that appropriate action will result; and, finally, to make clear that civil suits regarding defamation of character are not within your province, but within the domain of civil authorities. It is possible, indeed likely, that an internal inquiry will sail into becalmed waters. Proof from either side is not apt to surface. Any AAUP worth its dues will be quick to remind you, though you need no reminding, that no one should be judged guilty based on hearsay and unsubstantiated allegations. This to-do is apt to lead to multiple results: a significant amount of gossip that will, unfortunately, further damage the reputation of the School of Business and Economics; a transfer of the two students to another section of the same course or a faculty board review and evaluation of the students' work; and a reminder to Professor Y. about the dangers inherent in faculty-student relationships of a nonprofessional nature.

Your far from pedestrian responsibilities, however, center upon inducting into the academic culture a large number of junior faculty members in departments where the senior faculty are incapable or unwilling to act as mentors. To conclude that Professors W. and Y., with their various degrees of guilt, will have learned from this experience simply will not do. As Samuel Beckett at his satirical best in *Malone Dies* has made us understand, "To know you can do better next time, unrecognizably better, and that there is no next time, and that it is a blessing there is not, there is a thought to be going on with." These events should have reawakened you to the fact that if young faculty members are allowed to fumble toward the light, the dean will be forced to spend an undue amount of his time investigating skirmishes instead of providing leadership in achieving the excellence the university seeks.

This episode should also have reminded you that academic excellence depends primarily, not on image makers, publicists, and public relations experts, but on faculty—on their scholarship and their teaching. And while many young faculty members arrive on a campus clutching newly minted Ph.D.s that have prepared them to teach all there is to know about the right wing of the butterfly, few know much about the actual art of teaching and even less about acceptable behavior in dealing with their students. In matters of such proper academic behavior, one should never underestimate the naivete of very bright, highly educated 26 year olds whose yearly calendar has always begun the day after Labor Day. And while the code of the academic tribe is frequently quickly learned in well-established, reputable departments with strong chairs and generous senior faculty, here is an instance when a formal, ongoing, and extensive orientation program for young faculty is called for. In addition, every effort should be made to appoint your junior faculty from the School of Business and Economics to university-wide committees so as to introduce them to the views and manners of faculty from the institution's other and better grounded colleges. Thus, over a period of time, the young faculty so oriented should create an environment within the school that will eliminate the need for an unusually formal and extensive induction of new members into its institution.

Experience may be a good teacher, but it's occasionally late for class.

CHAPTER TWELVE
A COPY OF THE COMPLAINT IS ENCLOSED

A CASE OF DISCRIMINATION

When erected in San Francisco in 1891 the Crocker Building, astonishingly 11 stories high, was, according to the California historian Kevin Starr, the largest commercial building in the state. That same year many a university, whose present administrative offices with their thousands of almond-colored filing cabinets and mainframes and PC's and disc storage cabinets might just squeeze into the Crocker Building if it rented nearby space for its attorneys, certified public accountants, auditors, and assistants to the assistant deans, probably directed its enterprise from one floor of a Jacobean building. The relative newness of paper storms both in commerce and in academe with accumulations that often block out windows and doors and that occasionally result in avalanches that threaten to bury everyone leads both to thoughts of the ephemeral nature of our efforts and to the fear that the phenomenon is the result of some serious offense committed against Zeus. Surely Man would not deliberately call these storms down upon his own unprotected head.

However, though administrators may fear long paper trails and forms filed in triplicate, they fear lack of supporting evidence even more. While they can imagine what Saturday Night Live could do with a person whose title is "Coordinator of Forms," they can picture with even less effort what a plaintiff could do to a defendant without a manila-folder breastplate. There are undoubtedly many reasons for the extravagant growth of paperwork and bureaucracy in all its manifestations in colleges/universities, but assuredly fear of litigation is one of them.

Among the increasing number of faculty members who resort to courts of law or to commissions instituted to protect human rights in order to challenge the substance of judgments rendered by faculty colleagues and/or administrators many charge discrimination on the basis of race, sex, or national origin. Some of these claims are based on fact, others on fancy, but all involve complex

perceptions and long histories. In a culture where antidiscrimi-
nation laws and the will to observe them are fairly recent and
where Freudian interpretation or misinterpretation of human responsibility has at times operated as an extension of Calvinistic
determinism, it is difficult at best for any member of a minority
group to distinguish between paranoia and other personal short-
comings and to be certain where the border between social accountability ends and his own begins. Furthermore, since self-
assessment even under ideal circumstances can be painful and
involved, most would gladly substitute the assessment of others.

He, for example, has witnessed many an Anglo-Saxon view
with a jaundiced eye anyone not from the banks of the Thames.
She, on the other hand, has been called "doll" by the chair of the
department at a professional meeting. Their mothers have warned
them not to trust outsiders; their therapists have encouraged them
to be more assertive; their political associates have taught them
to say "No more." Without a doubt and with or without solid
evidence both can be perfectly sincere in alleging that only bigots
or chauvinists would deny them reappointment, or tenure, or
promotion. Meanwhile those who do the denying have breathed
the same often toxic air; been reared by equally protective mothers;
are trying to stop feeling guilty when they say "No"; and consider
it cowardly to succumb to what they perceive to be bullying. They
too in all sincerity consider their judgments to be essentially pure.
At times only the truth of a cliché will do: The situation is a human
one.

However, sincerity on both sides does not alter the fact that
complaints lodged against a college/university in offices of human
rights or suits alleging defamation or discrimination before courts
of law can be exceedingly time-consuming, often costly, and nearly
always conducive to heightened tension under the pressure of
"proving" honorable motives and compiling supporting evidence.
In addition, unless you are driven by temperament to beat your
9-year-old daughter at Monopoly, winning may well taste as gritty
as ashes. Meanwhile, even heavy-duty copiers collapse under the
strain and files grow in size and importance.

THE BACKGROUND

While other branch campuses of flagship state universities often
attempt to overcome identity crises, yours in northern New Eng-

land has enjoyed from the very beginning of its 22-year history a character distinguished by its location and its student body. Built in an era when the problem du jour was growth, it has benefited from the continued and dedicated support of the 30,000 towns-people as well as that of the citizens of a cluster of neighboring villages and one city which the Chamber of Commerce describes as a gathering of 100,000 who know how to live both in its clearing and in its surrounding woods and streams. The state university's main campus a comfortable 150 miles away spends little effort upstaging you and your enterprises, and the only other institutions of higher education in the area are a community college and a small denominational college for women, neither of which have ever shaken your stable 6,500 FTES or interfered with the full occupancy of your two 600-bed residence halls.

Ninety-eight percent of your students are natives of a state whose harmlessly chauvinistic population considers long absences as eccentricity or yet another manifestation of the folly of youth. The vast majority of your students are also of French Canadian descent. At the end of the nineteenth century their ancestors had bartered the harsh life of the Province of Quebec potato farms and lumber camps for the equally harsh life of cotton mills and shoe factories. Seduced by the same consumer dreams as some who had crossed oceans, they had followed the iron horse's tracks to tend machines instead of land.

Though on occasion Yankees still speak of marrying "French girls"; though "French girls" still think that dating a "Protestant" is worthy of mention if not forgiveness; though grandparents still refer to native New Englanders as "Americans," the immigrant's malaise and tensions have all but disappeared. This generation of Duboises and Daigles and Archambaults, and Bouchards manage banks as well as spindles, write dissertations on T. S. Eliot as well as on Marie Claire Blais, so that, finally, "home" sets off even deeper emotional reverberations than *chez nous*.

THE HAPPENING

In the family of modern languages taught at the university, French is the favored daughter for several reasons. One, since it is still spoken and even occasionally read in the bilingual homes of the community, it is not foreign in any challenging sense. A student is unlikely to be threatened by a language in which his grandmother's soaps are transmitted via cable every weekday afternoon. Two, while it lacks the exoticism of, say, Russian or Chinese, it feeds on ethnic pride at a time when French style is equated with sophistication and is influencing yuppie American culture in everything from high couture to high cuisine. And, three, now that practicalness has replaced cleanliness next to godliness, it is simply good business to perfect your bilingualism in a bilingual geographical area in which one hopes to sell goods or to render services. Hence, not only do students in the humanities fulfill their language requirement by registering for courses in French grammar, conversation, culture, and literature, but students electing preprofessional majors target this language as an investment of choice.

Three tenured faculty have until this fall attempted to meet all of the students' requests for courses. Professor A., attracted to your campus by its proximity to northern New England beaches that remind him of his native Normandy, is the senior member of the group. He is a kindly, diffident, disappointed, and lonely man who finds solace in books, yearly trips to Bayeux, and an addiction to Gauloises the fumes of which forecast his every arrival. He is dedicated to his students, who are not only grateful for his devotion but for his lack of pretense. Professor B., a native of the provinces who studied in the capital and eagerly returned home, is a man of 40 whose sensitivities are keen enough to interpret literature with insight but not so intense as to precipitate a midlife crisis. He is a boyish, enthusiastic, fun-loving person who drinks experience in large draughts and who as a consequence is loved and admired by his students. Professor A. is amused by him and warms his chilled soul by his blazing fire. Professor C., a woman well past the age when she might wonder which of divergent paths to follow, is harmlessly and amusingly dotty. With her outré dress and fey manners she seems held to earth only by the weight of her considerable knowledge. She is the kind of teacher responsible for college lore and anecdotes shared in dormitory rooms and Thanksgiving family gatherings. Professor A. and Professor B. conspire to protect her, but are never quite sure from what. In a word, these three form a compatible and happy subgroup within an unusually congenial Department of Modern Languages wherein the tenured faculty assume the chairmanship on a 3-year rotating schedule. The present chair, in office less than a year and for the first time, is an accommodating and somewhat timid but fun-loving and erudite *bon vivant* who teaches popular courses in Italian literature.

Since the courses in French are oversubscribed, you give the department permission to hire an additional instructor. In early spring the search committee proposes appointing Doctor X. a Parisian married to an American medical doctor who following specialized training abroad has recently established a practice in the area. Her degree is from the Sorbonne, and though she has but 1 year of teaching experience at an international school in Belgium, the committee is impressed by her publication record on esoteric medieval texts and possibly overly charmed by her elegance and her confidence.

You meet her briefly and are equally struck by her quite extraordinary presence. The tasteful and studied grooming, the modulated and cultured voice of a Texaco opera commentator, the graceful slimness, which attached to anyone over 30 you like to dismiss as affectation, are all far removed from your ordinary blue-book world. Her Dior scarf held in place by a modest pin makes you wish you had worn your better tweed and you find yourself inexplicably annoyed with the cigarette ash powdering Professor A.'s lapels. The latter interprets her Pinter-like silences as manifestations of profundity; you find them slightly unnerving and possibly indicative of a dangerous hauteur. However, the search committee and the chair of the department are enthusiastic, the credentials are in order, there is no solid reason to substitute your judgment for the judgment of the faculty, and there are six stops to tenure. You offer her an assistant professorship, which she accepts and the train begins to roll.

From the very first semester signs point to a bumpy ride. In early November all 18 students in Dr. X.'s Intermediate French conversation class sign the following letter addressed to the chair of the department.

Dear Dr. Y.:

We believe that as chair of the Department of Modern Languages you should be made aware of the following intolerable conditions in Dr. X.'s class in French Conversation.

We went into this course looking forward to learning to speak better a language that most of us speak at home. After only a week Dr. X's sarcasm and cold manner had nearly all of us scared to open our mouths. She laughs at what she calls with a sneer our "Canuck" accent. That's like calling a Jew a "Kike." She spent one whole period having us roll "r's" because that's the way they do it in Paris.

The topics for our class conversations are always chosen by her and usually ridiculous and stupid. As an example, last week's assignment was to discuss why the Bois de Boulogne in Paris is a more civilized city park than New York's Central Park. None of us had seen this park in Paris and only eight of us had ever been to New York. One girl who had never been out of New England got angry and defended Central Park and Dr. X. made fun of her in front of everybody. We were all scared to say anything because we don't want to flunk.

Maybe you can do something about this or maybe you can't, but the whole thing is unfair.

We want you to know though that this is the first time any of us are unhappy about a course in this department. Everybody else is friendly and cares about us.

Sincerely,

Intermediate French Conversation Class

The recently appointed chair of the Department of Modern Languages made nervous by his inexperience and by his distaste for conflict meets with you in mid-November and seeks guidance. Since all experiences as chair had been for him in the past year first draft events, he confesses to having provided Dr. X. with a perfunctory orientation and he has every intention of correcting that mistake. In addition, Professors A., B., and C., having received numerous student complaints about the course in question and others, are most willing to help though they have become somewhat shy in offering aid due to rebuffs received in response to earlier advances. Dr. X. has agreed to join the three of them for lunch early next week. All four, the chair and the three professors of French, are confident that once she understands the students' cultural background and sensitivies, she is certain to change ways that are unintentionally offensive. It is simply a matter of acclimatization, for she is a very intelligent woman. The correlation between intelligence and wisdom is not quite as clear to you as it is to the chair, but you support his nurturing attitude and envy his faith in the miracles that can be accomplished through goodwill.

At the end of this initial semester the chair examines the results of the official student evaluation of courses given by the university every fall term. Dr. X. comes out badly bruised. Her scores are by far the worst in a department that however is admittedly both popular and highly respected by the student body. The unofficial (non university-sanctioned) Student Government Association booklet, *Survival Guide*, which purports to review course offerings and to offer advice on what to pursue and what to avoid, is both succinct and direct in its assessment of *French 301: Intermediate French Conversation:*

> Picnic in Beirut; take snapshots of demonstrations in South Africa; draw American flags on the Kremlin walls. But if you value your life, don't take a course with Dr. X.

Well, even a chair in pursuit of peace must conclude that Dr. X. is certainly off to a poor start. However, he continues to believe that once she understands the campus and its students everything will undoubtedly improve. Students will come to appreciate, as some of the faculty already do, someone whose standards call for the best in all of us and whose scholarship deserves emulation. Just last month she had yet another paper accepted in a prestigious journal and read her most recent at the annual meeting of the Modern Language Association.

On February 15 Professor C. writes the chair a cryptic note. You receive a copy.

> Henceforth I will not under any circumstance recognize the presence of Dr. X. nor will I ever reveal the reasons for this decision.

Surely puzzles have their merits and their fun, but you are too busy helping to prepare for the legislative budget hearings to unravel the mysteries of anything but books that must balance.

A week and a half later the departmental rank committee votes 6–2 to recommend reappointment of Dr. X. for a second year but with the following expressions of concern, which are mailed to her and placed in her permanent file.

1. While student evaluations of courses are but one means of judging a faculty member's effectiveness in the classroom, repeated ratings significantly below that of the department's norm would be viewed as a matter of serious concern.

2. While Professor B.'s report of his two visits to her classes last semester was undoubtedly justified in its very high praise of her scholarship, its criticism of her authoritarian even intimidating tone and perhaps excessively remote manner had given the committee pause.

3. While the department would not expect a first-year faculty member, busy in the preparation of new courses and in acquainting herself with new colleagues, and new campus culture, to work on committees, it did hope that a second-year citizen would begin to participate in the workings of a shared governance system of which the university is proud.

On March 10 Dr. X., at her request, meets with you for a very long and very tense hour. In impeccable prose, nearly distracting in its complex and beautifully balanced feats, you are given the Parisian view of your imperfect universe. The chair of the Department of Modern Languages is an inept little man to whom standards of excellence are foreign. All three of the others who teach French are beyond salvation. Professor A. is a provincial with a Norman accent. Professor B. who visited her classes is unfit to judge her teaching for two reasons: one, he has published nothing since he dismembered his dissertation and sent the parts through the mails; two, his French/Canadian accent would never pass muster in a literary French world. Professor C., admittedly knowledgeable, considers a celebration of the Feast of St. John the Baptist at the parish hall a cultural event. The poor creature was offended, but one could not help laughing at her account of this event. Then, the students have been and continue to be encouraged to pursue mediocrity so, obviously, they will resent anyone who abhors it. Most importantly, and what you must be made to see, is that what is operative here is rank discrimination based on national origin. From the very first week of classes she had detected animosity directed against her because she is French from France and because, to her dismay, nay, to her shock, she had been obliged to defend the purity of the French language before colleagues who were at first amused and, then, hostile. For example, after having given a lecture on grammar in which she showed that French/Canadian locutions were in many instances a corruption of French as it should be spoken, she found this unsigned note taped to her door:

"Pure French is impure Latin."

Her husband, whose name is Armstrong, is as unbelieving as she is in the face of such attitudes, and her meetings with the members of the department while she was a candidate had led her to expect gratitude not hostility and certainly not reprisal. She is prepared to do her work in a conscientious manner and prepared to defend at whatever cost appropriate academic standards, but she is not prepared to tolerate bigotry and discrimination. She will defend herself with vigor. Of that you have no doubt.

Certainly there is no room in Dr. X.'s life for McCroissants, but you attempt to explain that her success at the university depends in part on her making some space for the culture that inspired them and for those, imperfect though they be, who enjoy them. A community that watches French/Canadian dramas on cable television, that sings "O Canada" after the U.S. national anthem at ballgames, that speaks Franglais in its homes and malls, is not going to take kindly to a ridiculing of its accommodations in languages, especially when that language nurtures much of its humor and its warmth. The faculty you are certain are in agreement: A literary French must be the French of the classroom. However, a literature that does not take into account a language that lives encourages aridity and a rigidity that, you have been told, the faculty find unattractive. The chair and the faculty have your confidence and you hope that as she gets to know them better they will gain hers.

You are not persuaded that any of your arrows have pierced Dr. X.'s armor. You file candid notes on the meeting, which you recount to the chair by phone and in more diplomatic terms. He is also careful in his response not to betray his weakening conviction that the marriage will endure, but for the first time a certain flatness in the voice gives him away.

The following fall's official student evaluations of Dr. X.'s courses show ratings that have improved slightly but not significantly, and the Student Government Association's remarks are no less terse, no less dismissive than they had been a year ago. A simple phrase is attached to *French 403, Medieval Literature:* "Skull and Crossbones."

Since Professor C., a woman of her word, steadfastly refused to acknowledge the existence of Dr. X., Professors A. and B. had accepted the unenviable task of visiting the probationary faculty member's classes on two separate occasions apiece. In sum their reports matched the previous year's conclusions. Dr. X., a highly cultured, beautifully educated, impressively scholarly woman had been unable or unwilling to establish harmonious relations with her students. Indeed, one of the four classes visited had in very few minutes (perhaps in honor of the visiting professor's presence) degenerated into a particularly tense and acrimonious debate regarding the now common usage of English terms when speaking French. The students, with vengeful pleasure, pointed out that the French/French delight in such words as "le jogging," "le software," and "le video clip," and that they and their families as French Canadians had been indulging in the same custom for years—had probably taught the Parisians a lesson. Dr. X., siding predictably with the Academie Française, the High Commission on French Language, and other French language purists who welcome foreign influences with as much enthusiasm as a foreign crossing of their borders, transformed by means of disdain a potentially stimulating intellectual discussion into a peasant revolt.

On the last week of February, the departmental rank committee votes regretfully but unanimously (8–0) to deny Dr. X. reappointment for the following year. When so informed by the chair, Dr. X. leaves his office without a word. A little over a month later, before you act upon the recommendation, you receive a document that you had been expecting: the Equal Employment Opportunity Commission wishes to inform you that Dr. X. has filed a complaint against the university and that you must respond in writing within 20 days to allegations of discrimination against her on the basis of her French national origin.

You barely have time to sigh before a very distraught chair of the Department of Modern Languages shares with you another similarly official-looking letter, which, however, you had not anticipated. You clear your way through the undergrowth of legal jargon only to be rewarded with another threat. Attorney G.L., a partner in a prominent local law firm, wishes the chair to understand that her client, Dr. X., has resorted to the law of defamation in order to challenge the substance of judgments he has rendered against her. Allegedly, not only has he attacked her professional competence in an effort to persuade the rank committee to deny her reappointment, but he has damaged her reputation in the community by recounting with malice at a party on December 23 certain classroom incidents that when thus parodied amounted to slander.

The Equal Opportunity Employment Commission hopes that the university's response will include a resolution acceptable to all parties involved, and attorney G.L. is certain that once the university fully understands the harm done to her client it will cooperate in seeking just restitution. In these instances "resolution" and "restitution" should more than likely translate as "reappointment."

The chair, a softball player and an inexperienced one at that, is stunned. Why would anyone throw that hard? No, he had not had to persuade a rank committee to dismiss Dr. X. Every member was only too happy to do so in order to restore the peace and harmony that her arrival had disturbed. No, he did not have a verbatim record of the minutes of the meeting at which the vote was taken. The members of the department trust one another and keep only action minutes. Yes, he may have, after a few trips to the wassail bowl, turned entertainer, but it was all quite innocent. He cannot remember the precise details. Come on, who could after 3 months? Well, you have not yet acted upon the recommendation of the department and you can always overturn it. If you really think about it, maybe the department should be big enough to accommodate one absolutist. Maybe everyone has behaved precipitously. Perhaps if given another chance, Dr. X. could solve her problems. It is not as if Dr. X.'s scholarship were in question. The students could learn a great deal from her and it may be time to stop coddling them. They are certain to meet such types in graduate school. The university provides no liability insurance for its chairs and it cannot expect them to be sued and to lose their homes because it will not tolerate a faculty member who is unpopular. He had never wanted the chairmanship of this department anyway. He had accepted a draft only out of a sense of civic obligation. He most certainly had not accepted the position for its attendant rewards. He has slid off the bobsled in midride and you find yourself having to regain your balance.

SUGGESTED COURSE OF ACTION

Deny reappointment and do so for the following reasons. One, though no one has faulted either Dr. X.'s scholarship or her general ability to share knowledge with students, virtually everyone concerned has deplored her narrowness of views, her lack of respect for intellectual positions that differ from her own, and her disdain for a culture that forms the background of a significant number of the university's students. Two, the prognosis for improvement is dismal, for well-meaning and well-disposed colleagues' attempts to help her have met nothing but resistance for three semesters. Three, her rigidity and arrogance have lost her the esteem of her colleagues. Four, she herself has been outspoken in expressing a lack of regard, even a contempt, for the other members of the department. In a university with a setting and a mission such as yours, collegiality and cordiality play major roles. Responsibilities of citizenship therefore call for certain attitudes and sympathetic responses toward faculty and students that might well be optional elsewhere. For example, Dr. X. could possibly be better suited to a research university in a state where a license tag reading "Je me souviens" is rarely seen and even more rarely noticed. She may well have come to you in the first place only because she had decided against a commuter marriage. One would have to admit, however, that her narrowness of vision would likely always find a means of expression. Five, there is no evidence of discrimination against her on the basis of national origin or any other basis. Indeed, by its very nature the Department of Modern Languages is not only receptive to foreign cultures but dedicated to promoting an understanding and appreciation of their differences. In her inability to respect the Franco-American patois and the French-Canadian language, the very heart of a people's culture, Dr. X. is guilty of the very weakness of which she accuses others.

The hiring of Dr. X. had simply been a mistake in judgment. It is far better to acknowledge a wrong turn immediately and to attempt to correct the error without delay than to forge ahead and hope that east will meet west. Dr. X.'s publications had been impressive; her Vogue style somewhat blinding. But if paper credentials and first impressions infallibly led to perfect and lasting unions between universities and individuals, one could argue for instant tenure. Probation means probation.

The Equal Employment Commission is unlikely to find reasonable cause to believe that the university has discriminated against Dr. X. However, before the matter is tucked away in files you may wish that the department had chosen means other than action minutes as opposed to a comprehensive record of its rank committee hearings to demonstrate its long-standing harmony. The birth of the 914 Xerox copier in 1960 and the subsequent birth of younger siblings have not only made possible the multiple duplication of billions of documents a year, but enlivened sociological speculation. Without Xerography would the world know fewer claimants? With fewer claimants would the world support less Xerography? Courts and Human Rights Commissions have in some cases behaved as if such questions were subversive. Lack of thorough documentation tied to all actions as tin cans to a dog's tail (to borrow from Yeats) seems at times to be equated with secrecy and secrecy with slithering in dark alleys. For example, in 1985, when a French instructor filed a discrimination complaint against Franklin and Marshall College, the 3rd U.S. Circuit Court of Appeals ordered the college to provide the EEOC with recommendations, evaluations, memoranda, and other documents related to all tenure candidates since 1977 (*EEOC* v. *Franklin and Marshall College*-84-1739). A lack of detailed record keeping including comprehensive minutes of relevant meetings might be viewed as negligent and/or might be judged as suspicious. In any event, whether or not the EEOC finds cause the plaintiff is given 90 days to file suit. The university's attorney is there to provide counsel, but it is good to remind yourself that the attorney's responsibilities do not include academic value judgments and decision making.

Dr. X.'s resorting to the law of defamation in order to challenge and/or punish the chair of the department is every bit as serious and considerably more complex a matter than is her filing a complaint of discrimination with the EEOC. In all cases where you find yourself thinking in such heroic terms as "the greater good of the university supersedes the good of the individual" take a lengthy and microscopic look at both your motives and the situation, for we all like to cut a fine figure and life stands us before such dramatic choices less frequently than our pride would allow us to believe. This is one case, however, when you are eye to eye with "my country or my friend" dilemma. You cannot impose an unsuitable faculty member upon a department and upon students in order to ward off the consequences of the chair's indiscretion; you cannot withdraw completely the university's support from a chair who has possibly behaved unprofessionally without unduly frightening all other chairs on campus and without the faculty concluding that one of their own has been abandoned. You will need all the wisdom and diplomacy at your command in steering a course between two shoals: that of the university's accepting blame for the chair's alleged defamatory expressions that exceeded the bounds of legitimate communication in the line of professional duty, and that of the university's callous forsaking of one of its own who may have danced in a crystal shop.

The reasons for the university's providing both legal counseling and moral support for the chair are not due solely to compassion and public relations. While academe in the past 20 years has paid considerable attention to the development of its faculty, only now is it awakening to the need to invest in the development of its midlevel administrators: its chairs of departments. In cases such as this one where a department enjoys a reputation for solid teaching, scholarly competence, and congeniality, the tendency is to engage in benign neglect until some breakdown attracts attention. You should seize this opportunity to institute an educational program for your department chairs that might include but not be limited to orientation sessions and workshops wherein experiences are shared and knowledge dealing with such legal matters as immunity, indemnity, law of defamation, liability insurance, the keeping of essential records and documents are made clear. Such sessions should also provide bibliographies in the rich literature of academic administration and draw attention to such helpful publications as "The Department Advisor," a quarterly under the directorship of the American Council on Education, which covers topics such as the role of the department chair in faculty evaluation, successful proactive recruiting strategies, and reducing the risk of legal liability.

Pay for your mistakes immediately; time will only inflate the cost.

CHAPTER THIRTEEN
MY PLATONIST HAS NOT MASTERED PLATO

A CASE OF UNQUALIFIED FACULTY

Classicists stroll the paths of academe; computer scientists walk the halls of the local high-tech park. Meanwhile, more and more freshmen arrive on American campuses each year wanting to prepare to enter that park and will not, unless forced by general university requirements, explore the Cave. Hence, most universities, either compelled by the marketplace or convinced by visions of a postindustrial age, have by now established Departments of Computer and Information Sciences. However, the American student's love of machines and his fear (often induced and certainly exacerbated by advertising agencies seeking to sell Apples) of entering the future as a computer "illiterate" have inflated the demand for computer science courses to a level that many institutions simply cannot meet. Consequently, attendant problems range from the difficulty of procuring expensive hardware in times of fiscal constraint, to staffing round-the-clock computer laboratories, to paying the high cost of maintenance contracts, to investing in equipment that is apt to become obsolete shortly after it has been installed. But the most serious problem of all centers upon computer science faculty. In a word, where to find them and what to do if you cannot.

THE BACKGROUND

Three years ago, after prolonged informal discussions in the Faculty Club and formal debates in the university senate, the Department of Mathematics and Computer Science concluded that the one should live as two. The Bill of Divorce specified that mathematicians or faculty in other disciplines who wanted visiting privileges in the newly formed Department of Computer and Information Sciences would be allowed to teach certain lower division courses providing they were actively pursuing an M.S. in

137

computer science to add to their Ph.D.s. Some grumbled about the arrogance of those who rode the crest of waves, and others cited this decision as yet another example of life's injustices, but most accepted this provision within the reorganization plan as sound for two reasons. One, the bona fide computer scientists sought to maintain the integrity of their discipline and the academic standards of their offerings. They feared that, since faculty trained in the computer sciences were both difficult to attract and to hold, the temptation to assign classes to mathematicians or physicists who enjoyed playing with a PC on weekends might be too alluring to resist. And, two, a research university within short commuting distance offered graduate degrees in computer science.

While the reorganization has not been free of problems, it is now, 3 years later, generally described as successful. Two mathematicians and one physicist, aided by university grants, are close to the completion of an M.S. in computer science; 600 computer science majors are fairly content. However, the problem of staffing continues to plague both the chair of the department and the dean of the College of Natural and Mathematical Sciences and is now affecting faculty morale. In the heady first 3 years of its newly declared independence, in the days of designing new letterheads, rearranging offices, and establishing its own governance structure, all members of the department accepted a seat on the faculty search committee with eagerness, for most were convinced that practices of the past had been neither aggressive nor creative enough to build a strong faculty. But now that 3 years of aggressive and creative recruiting efforts have resulted only in moderate success, now that students all too often must still wait until their senior year to be admitted to certain electives, now that as many as 500 students majoring in fields other than computer science are turned away each semester from lower division courses that they seek as electives, many are realizing that a flag does not a nation make.

Reality has taken the most comfortable chair in the Faculty Club, and faculty grumbling fills the air.

"My classes are too large."

"Instituting a screened major has not had much impact."

"The provost is placing even more emphasis on publications for promotion, and I'm spending my time recruiting colleagues."

"How can so few of us continue to advise so many students."

"We have so much to do in the department that we have no time left to run for membership on university-wide committees, and, so, we have no impact on policies. Some shared governance."

"Why should I put up with this when I can make twice as much in salary 10 miles from here at G.E."

THE HAPPENING

It is July 29 and you have already bought green docksiders for that week in Maine. The fall term begins one month from today. Morale in the Department of Computer and Information Sciences has risen one notch because one Ph.D. and one A.B.D. in the field have said that, after weighing all offers, they had decided to sign the contracts you had mailed them for the coming year. No one in that department has resigned. Last spring, the board of trustees had approved a differential salary scale for computer scientists and nearly everyone has happily thrown themselves into the *post hoc ergo propter hoc* fallacy trap and are not even experiencing discomfort.

At 4:00 p.m. that day—Fate always sends bad news at 4:00 p.m. so that you may spend the evening worrying—the dean of Natural and Mathematical Sciences calls to say that Mr. X., the A.B.D. in computer science who had said he would sign a contract for the fall term, had also made the same promise to two other universities. When confronted, he had made it clear that his intention was to sign only one contract, but that that one was not yours. Here was a man who clearly knew his worth on this side if not the next. The conversation ends with the dean saying, "I'll be sending you another contract for your approval, but you won't like it. I've kept it in the emergency file for a month."

He was right; you do not like it. Mr. Y., the candidate being recommended, however reluctantly, has taught computer science courses at a local community college for the past 3 years and has 2 years of experience operating a mainframe in industry. The part of the resume you do not like lists the credentials: a B.S. in chemistry and 15 credits toward M.Ed. in computer education. When you call the dean to express both surprise and concern (you are too experienced to express outrage), it becomes clear that he is under considerable pressure. The chair is threatening to resign if "the administration doesn't do something"; 128 students have registered for the four courses which our "man of worth" had agreed to teach; the dean of the School of Business and Economics, whose students are included among those registered, is beginning, after two glasses of Chablis, to use such words as "incompetence" and "mismanagement"; the mathematicians who never approved of the restructuring of the Department of Computer and Information Sciences are less than sympathetic; and 3½ weeks are left before the opening bell.

SUGGESTED COURSE OF ACTION

Refuse to offer a faculty contract to Mr. Y. and state your reasons both verbally and in writing to the dean, to the chair of the department, and even to the department itself if it becomes necessary to boost morale and your administrative style warrants it.

Expediency is not the queen of virtues, and it is very dangerous to treat her as such. Your image as an institution that seeks academic excellence is the most important bond in your portfolio, and if you sell it for short-term profit, you will learn in the long term that you had been paid a bowl of porridge in return.

This Department of Computer and Information Sciences had been founded, quite rightly, upon the principle that academic credentials affected both the substance and image of a program. Otherwise it would not have insisted that Ph.D.s in other fields, even those given to use of the computer in their work, such as mathematicians and physicists, were to add formal training in this relatively new discipline. And, notice, that it had not required the mathematician and the physicist simply to take courses in computer science, but actually to enroll in a structured program that led to a graduate degree. While a great deal of silliness has attached itself to the accumulation of credentials (such as refusing to allow native speakers without methods courses to teach foreign languages in secondary schools), there is no denying that the *sine qua non* of good teaching is knowledge of the subject matter, and that asking graduate schools to certify that one criterion has by and large been reliable. Listing the members of the faculty's degrees at the back of a university catalogue is not an exercise in vanity, but a way of telling the community that while credentials do not guarantee effective teaching, they do assert that specialists in the various fields have attested to the fact that the faculty know their disciplines.

To hire a person whose only earned degree is a B.S., even to teach solely lower division courses, would be to apply to outsiders criteria that are considerably lower than those applied to insiders; to harm the reputation of the Department of Computer and Information Sciences in the minds of the faculty in other departments who would be within their rights to demand an explanation; to harm the reputation of the university in the minds of students and their parents and friends who are well aware of the need for degrees and are paying tuition to prove it; and, finally, might well raise a question about the future within a university of a discipline that is so little theoretical that a B.S. and experience running a mainframe will suffice to teach undergraduates. Incidentally, remember that Mr. Y. is without a national reputation as a computer scientist. If he were, we would be dealing with a different case.

If all other options have been explored, you might consider hiring Mr. Y. as an assistant instructor who would help two or three faculty members run laboratories, grade quizzes, and lead discussion groups. In return, these faculty members might consent to assume added responsibilities for lectures, advising of students, and awarding of final grades. If no such agreement can be reached, all four lower division classes should be canceled.

Standards of excellence demand that what a university cannot do well, a university should not do at all.

CHAPTER FOURTEEN
A CURRICULUM FOR THE POOR
A CASE OF PROGRAM REVISION

In his short story, "Construction," Donald Barthelme's central character thinks as follows:

> Although I feel that much of what my father taught me, in his quite bold and dramatic way, his quite bold and dramatic and let it be acknowledged self-dramatizing way, was of great use to me later . . . although had he really loved me he would have placed more stress, perhaps, on air-conditioning, the manufacturing, sale, installation, and maintenance of air-conditioning.

Well, this fellow beset by regrets might find himself at home in an academic age where, for example, one state college's textile engineering department reportedly hauls a knitting machine through towns on the back of a truck and in an attempt to lure students to its vocational program knits socks for them in their school colors in return for their names and addresses.

That Secretary of Education William Bennett's faith in the value of the humanities for all students and that the Association of American Colleges' faith in "definition and rigor" in all curricula has reached for some administrators and faculty Mathew Arnold's "melancholy, long, withdrawing roar" has been made manifest by the need for a rash of national and regional reports from task forces calling for a reinstatement of a demanding study of the liberal arts to its former central place in the baccalaureate experience.

Before the Civil Rights Movement, before the Women's Movement, before the large immigration of Hispanics, and before colleges/universities began to question their frequently ungenerous, if not always unjust, admission policies, we as a people were generally agreed that however we defined an educated person, and whatever disagreements we might have about the two cultures, a college graduate was expected to be a cultivated person. And a cultivated person in this metaphorical sense suggested someone who had not been abandoned to his natural state—someone who had been cared for and nurtured. In a word, someone who had received the benefits of civilization. And the knitting of socks was simply beside the point.

Numerous and complex social and economic forces have eroded this conviction and/or rendered it for some too costly and too demanding to defend. As a consequence, a niggardly spirit, often disguised in a respectable power-blue suit of accountability, now walks the corridors of many universities and enters staff meetings unchallenged. How is your institution answering the immediate needs of the local accounting firms? Is your institution "producing" enough nurses? Too many historians? Every academic administrator is called to defend the need for new programs or the success of well-established ones before legislative committees and state boards with figures that trace the potential material success of potential students or alumni. Even some of the humanities, such as history, are defended on the grounds that an informed citizen is essential to a democratic nation. In many quarters "accountability" has become a euphemism for "return on investment." Vocationalism rides the waves and students, cheered by parents, hang on to it tightly for fear of drowning.

THE BACKGROUND

Your urban, public, 7,000 FTES comprehensive university is no old stone and moss oasis where Gucci-shod students read Aristotle beneath the soft light of stained-glass windows. It is a red-brick and plastic hustle and bustle sort of a place where the sons and daughters of blacks and of Korean, Hispanic, Russian, and Polish immigrants arrive by subway to gather knowledge and insight before boarding a bus that will carry them to Burger Kings and K-Marts for late afternoon and evening work shifts. Your campus, indistinguishable from the unimpressive apartment buildings that encircle it, shares with its neighbors a noisy tough world where meals are taken on the run, potential violence lurks behind doors, and only the energetic get to sit by the barely warm radiators in winter.

The majority of your students major in preprofessional programs: accounting, business management, computer science, medical technology, mass communication. Your alumni are employed; their parents seem pleased; your undergraduates seem not displeased. Your general university requirements were last revised in 1979 and are more accurately described as a soufflé than a curriculum. A pinch of this and a pinch of that and a dash of hope that once the concoction spends time in the oven it will rise. Faculty, 73% of whom are tenured, had read the demographic charts and had foreseen that a department unprotected by regulations that required students to take some of its offerings might well be deserted by the mid-1980s. Hence, the distribution requirements had been and still were spread thinly across a host of disciplines, not limited to the arts and sciences, on the grounds that all knowledge was worth having. Such a view had received the undivided support of a strong AAUP chapter. To attribute a crass motive to every member of the faculty who had voted with the majority might reveal an unjustifiably jaundiced view: Certainly some and perhaps many found themselves incapable of defending the merits of reading, say Soren Kierkegaard as opposed to Bernard Baruch, and others genuinely believed that process as opposed to content was the issue. In their view, any well-taught course could help a student learn to form judgments and to develop perspective. All disciplines were equally worth knowing.

The many hours of hearings and faculty senate debates had resulted in a close vote and wounds that the defeated who had argued for a core curriculum in the arts and sciences wore proudly as red badges of courage. Your predecessor, who had openly supported the losing side, had sighed and sought green pastures.

THE HAPPENING

Inspired by an increasingly vocal national criticism of the undergraduate intellectual experience and still smarting from the sting of being associated with a curriculum that they could not praise, those who had not taken the hill in 1979 now regrouped. Without fanfare so as not to awake the dozing and with a determination to avoid the strategic mistakes of the past, this group agrees upon a detailed and methodical plan to protect the undergraduates in an age of barbarism. Within 2 years they have elected enough sympathizers to the university senate and to the key University Curriculum Committee to make a well-conceived move. At the opening session of the senate in the fall when many are still feeling beach sand under their toes and nearly all are too preoccupied with the preparation of introductory lectures to read the agendas of upcoming meetings, a motion mandating the University Curriculum Committee to reexamine the general university requirements and to bring recommendations to the senate at its May meeting carries with little debate.

However, by the end of October the entire faculty has been alerted to the threat of change and the resulting debate is not limited to the open hearings scheduled by the curriculum committee. Departments devote hours of formal meetings to the topic; students report being subjected to classroom harangues on the snobbery of literati and the narrowness of accountants; philosophers and physical educators clash by noon in the cafeteria. You begin to receive threatening letters, warning letters, pleading letters, obsequious letters, silly letters, wise letters, and even one unsigned obscene letter. While your administrative style has always encouraged debate as part of academic inquiry, you now remember, perhaps too late, the fourth of Richard Strauss's Ten Golden Rules for a conductor: "Never look encouragingly at the brass."

In defense of the status quo:

> Look, we are now charged with educating the masses, not medieval monks. All that talk about decay in the undergraduate program that you deplore is not something I can take seriously. All right, I'll say what many think and don't dare say except to their friends. Why should students be required to read Shakespeare in this day and age? That was all right maybe before the days of access. Now we have Jews and Blacks and Women and Hispanics in colleges. It's a different world. Those kids don't need Shakespeare. They need to learn to read, and write, and count, and prepare for jobs. They're not here to get gentlemanly Cs while waiting to join their fathers' firms. They can't afford to spend two years out of four reading poetry and playing games about what you do with four people in a lifeboat when there's only enough food for two. Besides, I said it in 1979 and I say it again: You have no proof that a course in medieval history is more important for our students than a course in computer science. Our graduates have to compete for entry level jobs after four years here and they won't be able to do that if you force 50 some odd credits of arts and sciences on them when what they want is to get into marketing or work in a hospital lab or teach in an elementary school. The people who sat on these national task forces whose reports you're eager to quote come from Columbia, and Berkeley, and Washington U., and Hood, and the U. of Chicago. They don't come from a poor AASCU institution. Bennett should spend a month with us.

In defense of change:

I'll tell you what you're arguing for. You're arguing for an in-
ferior curriculum for the poor, the minorities, and the disad-
vantaged. Why should we design a curriculum for the poor?
Why should we be preparing our students for entry level jobs
only? Why should the moments of heightened consciousness
occasioned by truly seeing because someone taught you to see
the windows of the Sainte-Chapelle be the domain of the leisure
class? Why should the turn of a phrase, the structure of an argument, the allusions to the past, the music of a poem, make
only those of a privileged background feel intensely alive? I do
not recall that when my friends and I were being reared by poor
French-Canadian and European immigrants in small New England towns in the 1940s and 1950s any of our elders were particularly concerned about what we would *do* either for them or
for our country. But, without having read a word of Sartre,
everyone seemed to be passionately caring about what we
would *be*. The joy my friends and I took in challenging one
another with passages from Corneille was never denigrated as
of little use to the seriously ailing cotton mills that lined our
rivers and in which our parents and our grandparents worked.
As it turned out, however, many of us did *do* quite a bit, in
part, out of gratitude to a nation that did not view us as an
investment, and, in part, out of admiration for a faculty whose
generosity of spirit was exemplified one day in the words of
my English teacher when I was 14: "I remember how wonderful
it was to read Jane Austen for the first time. I'm so happy for
you that you are about to have that experience." I understood
the words then; I understand their meaning now. That faculty
member would certainly have been perplexed by our placing
in newspapers ads designed to entice undergraduates to register
for our paralegal studies because x% will be needed by the year
2000. I don't doubt that you mean to do well by our students
and I don't doubt that you care. But you are dead wrong about
what we should do for them.

So it goes. And beneath the waves of rhetoric swims a large fish
to which no one dares draw attention, but upon which everyone
keeps a frightened eye: the effect on enrollment by discipline occasioned by any change in the general university requirements. At least
two non-Arts and Sciences departments fear being forced to retrench
tenured faculty if a revised curriculum eliminates their disciplines
from satisfying either a core or distribution requirement.

Meanwhile, the AAUP, like a poor bird perched on a piling
and not knowing which way to fly (to paraphrase Saul Bellow),

stands now on one leg now on another in an attempt, one, to defend the laudable principle that the determination of an appropriate curriculum is the responsibility primarily of the faculty, and, two, to avoid the choppy waters of retrenching faculty for financial exigency.

By January not even the holidays have lifted the dread with which all those not clad in armor await the May meeting of the senate now referred to as a performance entitled, "Sometimes the Dragon Wins."

SUGGESTED COURSE OF ACTION

Few universals govern administrative decisions, which should be free to turn at the flick of a circumstance. However, in this dangerous case perhaps two apply. The first is that no curriculum however splendidly designed will meet its objectives without the enthusiastic support of the faculty. The second is that stripped of eloquence, subtlety, data, and arcane references, convictions regarding curricula always give evidence of having been inspired less by books than by life. Unlike, say, entrepreneurs in the marketplace whose self-esteem may actually be raised by the thought of having succeeded without the support of an impressive educational preparation, academicians profess to know rather than to do and their concept of self-worth is intimately related to the perceived degree of intellectual demands placed upon them by curricula of the past. Hence, it is essential to remember that when a faculty member with three degrees in occupational therapy none of which required a knowledge of classical languages hears a Miltonian accuse the university of conferring undergraduate degrees upon barbarians who cannot read Latin and Greek that faculty member's response may be judged controlled if it does not include violence. All by way of saying that in higher education disputes regarding curricula are among the most complex, for what influences rational discourse is not simply the fear of decisions that might weaken job security, but the terror of conclusions that might diminish one's professional and personal view of self.

An understanding of the preceding should support tolerance and civility, but it should not eliminate convictions, whatever their provenance. Not all knowledge is of equal importance and no curriculum should be structured solely to meet the immediate needs of a community or dictated solely by the short-term interests of uneducated and inexperienced students. It is to the benefit of everyone for administrators to hold strong even passionate views about what it means to be educated and to exercise a leadership that promotes those views. Only thus do universities develop personalities that are distinguishable from that of others, and only then are students and their parents given choices not limited to the rate of tuition, the view from dormitory windows, and the scholarly reputation of faculty.

In the case with which we are now dealing, you know weeks before the spring term that a very serious situation is in the making. You must act now. You must not allow the benches to empty onto the field at the senate meeting in May because, and this is very important, even if you do manage to keep the controversy within acceptable bounds of academic behavior and bring about a compromise you will be perceived as a referee, as someone whose convictions regarding the heart of the enterprise are as firm as Jell-O. You may well be seen as the cause of both sides' defeat. You must act now even if your intent is to take some courageous stand at the May meeting, for you should not knowingly place yourself in a position of having to designate the knights and the dragons. You do not want a sizable number of faculty working with a curriculum that has been imposed on them even if it has been imposed by other faculty.

The consequences of your not succeeding in establishing a curriculum that has integrity and the support of the majority of the faculty are so serious that you should now put aside all non-essential projects and activities and direct all of your energies to exercising power through persuasion. Meet week after week with key individuals and small groups and gain pockets of support before attempting meetings with increasingly larger groups for the purpose of convincing all faculty of the following.

One, that since a university is its faculty, a seriously divided faculty is as dangerous to the health of a university as a divided personality is to the health of an individual. All faculty, out of idealism or self-preservation or love of peace, will opt for accord over discord if they do not have to sacrifice integrity.

Two, that to design a meta-curriculum has been the secret dream of all academicians in the Western world since Plato and Cicero. For one thing, a viable curriculum changes in order to keep pace with the intellectual advancements of an age. Otherwise, to quote Alfred North Whitehead, it "suffers the fate of all organic things that are kept too long." And for another, it is difficult not to love one's conclusions: We all seek an answer until we find one we like. Hence, the inclination to redesign our general university requirements in such a way that our G.U.R.s out-G.U.R. all other G.U.R.s is omnipresent.

Three, that a faculty might profitably begin designing or revising a curriculum by charting what it would like the certification of its students as "educated" to mean; that a faculty, however well intentioned, might operate from premises that have never been questioned.

Four, that in an age of anxiety such as ours department turf protection understandably temporarily blinds even the most idealistic and that such fears should be confronted. Consequently, you are now working with the AAUP and a special ad hoc committee of senior faculty to guarantee through contingency university-wide staffing plans and faculty development retraining and reassignment programs the job security of all tenured faculty. Representatives of the two departments feeling most threatened should be heavily involved in all of these contingency plans. It is unreasonable to ask any tenured faculty member not up for canonization to view as ideal a revision of G.U.R.s that might result in his professional demise. It is unreasonable to expect either a faculty to approve curricula revisions that will bring about the dismissal of tenured colleagues, or to expect a faculty that survive such a happening to ever work again in unity and trust.

Five, that in all universities, but especially in one such as yours, one should carefully distinguish between vocational and professional courses. That to label a course "liberal arts" is not thereby to guarantee its authenticity as a liberating course; that to label another "professional" is not thereby to assure its inability to provide perspective. Understandings between the two sides in question here might be more easily reached if all faculty resolved that each course given in a professional program be truly professional as opposed to narrowly vocational. That is, that it be structured in such a way that while it provided students with the body of skills essential to a particular field, it placed these skills within a political, environmental, historical, and ethical context. Ideally, every professional as, indeed, every course, whether it be in dance, marketing, physical education, or nursing would thus place events and theories within the context of man's long intellectual history, and every course, not only those in the arts and sciences, would thus contribute significantly to the liberal education of all students.

To conclude that one has adequately strengthened the undergraduate curriculum by requiring more courses in the arts and sciences, however necessary that may be under certain circumstances, is, nevertheless, to miss the spirit of the recommendations of all national task forces. Every preprofessional course in a university should, in addition to teaching required skills, seek the same ends as those that drive the liberal arts courses themselves, namely, to provide perspective, to hone judgment and imagination, and to challenge assumptions.

Thus, a course in industrial relations in the School of Business does not limit itself to an analysis of contract negotiations and legal constraints, but provides insights into the history of labor unions and encourages students to take a course in the history of American Labor. A course in the overview of physical education spends time on the sociology of sports and the role of sports in American and foreign cultures. Courses in early childhood and elementary education require an understanding of the latest findings in biology and psychology related to motivation, etc.

If every professional course on campus were henceforth guided by this spirit, you would have restored the liberal arts to a central place in the undergraduate curriculum without necessarily having increased significantly the number of credits in any one discipline. Take care. For this suggestion is but a piece of the whole. A significant number of courses in the arts and sciences are essential to the education of every student.

No faculty member in professional undergraduate programs wishes to deprive any student, including the minorities and the poor, of the intense pleasures of a cultivated life. However, a vocationally oriented curriculum can have precisely that effect. Many students have already been cheated in universities of what should have been theirs by right during 4 years that can never be revisited. The poor, whose parents are frequently in awe of college/university faculty and administrators and whose background has not prepared them to challenge the policies of academe, will frequently be satisfied, even grateful, for a narrow preparation for an entry-level job. Therefore, it falls upon those in positions of power in academe, those whose own lives have been transformed by a liberal arts education, to guard against constructing curricula that deceive the unsophisticated into believing that a B.A. stamped on just any course of study automatically confers upon it authenticity. To do otherwise is to engage in the educational version of sewing designer labels on shoddy goods.

Your short-term budgetary decisions and your long-term staffing plan should support programs of study that will prepare all who seek an enriched intellectual and cultural life the opportunity to live one. Every American youth should experience the joy of battling windmills, hunting a white whale, and meeting cyclops. In a land as wealthy as our own these joys should never be the exclusive rights of those who can buy the cultivation of self.

Not all curricula are created equal.

CHAPTER FIFTEEN
SEX: ITS MULTIPLE DISCOURSES
A CASE OF ACADEMIC LICENSE

In his *History of Sexuality* the French philosopher Michel Foucault contends that "what is peculiar to modern societies . . . is not that they consigned sex to a shadow existence, but that they dedicated themselves to speaking of it ad infinitum." Novelists describe it, historians trace it, psychiatrists probe it, pedagogues teach it, demographers predict it, and preachers warn against it. Where once only confessors and canonists made a living off it, entire professions have now dedicated themselves to analyzing it and to feeding modern man's insatiable curiosity regarding it. A person's truth about himself is equated to the truth about his sexuality. Sex for many has replaced the soul as the center of one's being. Consequently, sexual well-being has replaced spiritual health as a measure of one's worth.

Since no one, not even academicians, completely outstrides the postulates of his age, sex in its manifold aspects is a topic of study and discussion in virtually every discipline in the modern university: biology, education, psychology, literature, economics, business, history, sociology, in a word, every discipline with the possible exception of mathematics, where even there bad jokes about figures have been known to attempt a foray into the contemporary mode albeit tangentially.

While scholars debate the nature and causes and consequences of this preoccupation, and, thereby, ironically confirm it, virtually no one denies its legitimacy in the syllabi of courses across disciplines. However, two aspects of the study of sexuality, whether in biology, history, or literature, remain controversial: the choice and level of language used in lectures and encouraged in discussions that focus on it, and the tone that characterizes the instructor's general approach to the topic. The two aspects are, of course, inextricably linked.

THE BACKGROUND

Your Department of Anthropology is small: three full-time faculty members and 33 majors, but it attracts a significant number of students who choose its offerings as electives. The department is one of 16 in a regional college of liberal arts with a student FTE of 1,200 located in a small northern New England town. A kind, grandfatherly cultural anthropologist, who had some years back substituted long, rambling, uninspired discussions with students in and out of class for vigorous intellectual work in and out of class, retires after 30 years at the college. The search committee charged with finding his replacement, motivated in part by a fear of cloning, recommend a lively 27-year-old woman with a newly awarded West Coast Ph.D. and no teaching experience.

The young instructor's maiden semester is enviably successful. Her colleagues find her interesting and pleasant; the chair is relieved to see that she is cooperative without being fawning and enthusiastic without being flighty. She has brought just enough California with her to appear exotic to a student body whose homes line a cold gray coast, dreary back country roads, and polluted rivers that once provided power for cotton mills whose windows are now boarded. The removal of her leather coat before class is known as "the unveiling"; the head of the cafeteria has agreed to keep her supply of Perrier with lime in the refrigerator; and she has mounted on the walls of her office photographs of herself and of her husband, an amateur archeologist, in their Banana Republic clothes on digs in Egypt. Students of the 1960s might have denounced her for preferring the dead to the living. Students of the 1980s, in imitation of her, wear their watches with the crystal on the inside of their wrists as if protecting a Rolex from being scratched by the bone of a brontosaurus.

THE HAPPENING

At the end of the fall term, so many students preregister for this young woman's course, "Sex Roles in Cross-Cultural Perspective," that the chair, an orderly, meticulous man not given to welcoming changes, is obliged to rearrange not only her schedule, but his own and that of the third member of the department whose "Human Evolution and Pre-History" was undersubscribed for the first time in 5 years and had to be canceled. Both the chair and the

Third Man weather the incident, but both give signs of not en-joying even minor tempests.

Two months into the spring term, this promising instructor, perhaps whipped by what she views as acclaim, is rumored to have kicked over the traces: she is indulging a penchant for sa-lacious jokes and non-Victorian expletives while describing to her students the Assyrians' attitude toward sex. Some defend her as a delightful raconteur, while others accuse her of seeking popu-larity by pandering to students who take great pleasure in being shocked.

At the beginning of April, the Affirmative Action officer re-ceives the following letter. You and the chair of the anthropology department are copied.

Dear Mr. Y.:

I'm the one writing this, but many other students agree with me. I want to lodge a complaint about Dr. Paula Frame, who teaches "Sex Roles in Cross-Cultural Perspective."

My father and my uncle who have worked on the docks at the harbor all their lives don't use the foul language she uses in class and they certainly would not use it in front of girls. And here's a woman who says "Fuck" and "Shit" and some words that I don't even want to write down in a letter to you. She says them in almost every class. I didn't even know what the word "Schmuck" meant before taking this course.

Plus she tells jokes that embarrass me before my girlfriend who is also in this class. My girlfriend told me not to bother writing to you because it would only get me into trouble and you wouldn't do anything about it anyway.

I'm not naive. I know that it's the Profs who have all the power on campus. I'm also not innocent. I admit that at first I laughed the way many others did, but I'm a Christian and I now feel guilty that I laughed.

I'm a sophomore economics major and it's the first and last course I ever take in anthropology. In fact, I'm even dropping this one today.

You really should do something about this. I went to see the chair of my department, but it didn't do any good. If you can't do anything, maybe the chair of the anthropology de-partment can.

Sincerely yours,

Roger Tree

The student has attached to his letter a copy of the midterm examination and two quizzes that contain juvenile slang in referring to genitalia and questions punctuated with phrases of double entendre.

The situation, as nearly always, is complicated by the personalities of the combatants revealed in subsequent investigation.

The student not only demands that the lady go forth and sin no more, but, driven by a need to assuage his guilt at having hesitated many weeks to denounce her and at having feigned amusement (or really been amused) when his conscience dictated otherwise, now wants her to apologize to a class that is viewing the drama with interest. "Why shouldn't she be humiliated the way my girlfriend and I have been?"

The chair of the economics department did not believe when the student first came to him that he should interfere in another man's department and he has not changed his mind. Besides, such complaints are often exaggerated and if allowed to ripen unpicked, they just as often fall to an unreceptive soil, wither and die. "Why don't we cultivate a little laissez-faire and all that, don't you know?"

The chair of the anthropology department, still smarting from having to rearrange his spring schedule and that of his friend, the Third Man, is determined not to appear vindictive. He will speak to the instructor, of course, for he does not condone or defend such abuse of language. However, students should be made to understand that a good liberal arts education challenges all of your assumptions. You should be made to question every premise you hold dear including whatever absolute you have adopted governing the appropriateness of certain styles of speech in various settings. "Why can't we sit down over coffee and discuss this in a civilized way?"

The Affirmative Action officer, who is not as interested in feeding the hungry as he is in ending hunger, has discussed the matter at length with the student and advises you to reprimand the instructor in writing and to inform her that this reprimand now becomes part of her permanent record. Furthermore, were he in your place, and, of course, he is always thankful that he is not, he would ask the chair of the anthropology department to monitor the instructor's quizzes and examinations for appropriateness of language for the next 3 years. "Why can't we make it clear to this woman from the beginning that we treat our students with respect?"

Dr. Paula Frame when informed by the chair of the anthropology department of the complaint brought against her is outraged. The questions on her examinations refer to accurate descriptions of Ugaritic religion, and uninformed persons can have these facts confirmed by calling the leading authority on Semitic languages who is in the Department of Near Eastern Studies at a research university but a phone call away. Furthermore, if colloquial expressions offend some students and administrators, she can only point out that this is the way people talk outside of ivory towers. Besides, part of the intent of the humor, such as referring to the "grand brazziere" instead of the "grand vizier" is to break the tension of the examination. She did not make sex one of the major motivating factors in human beings. She did not cause many ancient religions to make sex a large part of their myth and ritual.

She does not deny using such words as "fuck" and "shit" in class; she insists on referring to them as "colloquial expressions"; and she characterizes her choice of them as contemporary and honest and free. She is only telling it like it is.

She is convinced that no complaint would have been registered if she were a man. Those who are offended are offended only because the words are being spoken by a woman. Apparently, jokes about sex are the prerogative of men. Well, she refuses to submit to this form of discrimination. Academic freedom allows her to teach her discipline using whatever means she finds effective.

Henceforth, she will add the following consumer warning to all of her syllabi:

> This course will contain numerous descriptions of sex and violence related to sex as well as honest colloquial language. If you are apt to be offended by this, you may wish to drop the course now.

In conclusion, Dr. Frame wondered whether we knew that Roger Tree had failed the midterm examination and both quizzes. "Why can't administrators save everyone time by defending a faculty member's academic rights without having to be prodded?"

SUGGESTED COURSE OF ACTION

Your first challenge is to cross this case without tripping any of the booby traps that lie all over the terrain. Let us uncover them in the order of their power to do serious harm.

Booby trap #1: Dr. Frame's use of profanity in class and sexual puns and jokes in examination questions are rights guaranteed by the principles governing academic freedom.

Nonsense. The principle of academic freedom, which must be defended at all cost, guarantees an academician's right to teach and to publish the results of his scholarship in his discipline. No one here is attempting to prevent the instructor from seeking truth in the *ars erotica* of the Arabic-Moslem societies or the "sex-positive" culture of the Indians of the Mehinaku tribe in Brazil or even the North American myths that associate sex with automobiles. In addition, while choice of methodology comes under academic freedom, Dr. Frame does not argue that her use of profanity and double entendre is a pedagogical route to any destination. She simply talks and jokes that way because according to her that is the way people talk in the real world.

Booby trap #2: Were Dr. Frame a man, there would be no case.

While few American males are comfortable using the word "cute" and American females avoid the word "cunt"; and while some feminists see this phenomenon as a lack of freedom for both sexes; and while sociologists and linguists can teach us a great deal about ourselves by examining such taboos, this case is not gender driven. Indeed, complaints very similar to the one brought against this female instructor are frequently lodged against male professors in American universities. Under these circumstances, the charges are most often viewed as a form of sexual harassment where the instructor takes pleasure in embarrassing and/or humiliating female students. It is highly likely that Dr. Frame's style would eventually have become a subject of controversy even if she had been a man though the conflict might have taken a sexual harassment turn.

Booby traps #3 and #4 have been placed close to one another. The student is failing the course and wants you to punish the instructor. The student feels guilty and if you punish Dr. Frame, he will have transferred his weakness onto her and restored himself to a state of grace.

Perhaps true, perhaps not, but surely irrelevant.

The pursuit of style in teaching as in all else is both sensible and honorable. Dr. Frame is to be commended for wanting to create one that is distinctive, but must also be made to understand that a style that distracts and/or offends succeeds only in sabotaging its own purpose: communication in all its forms. To ask an instructor to show the same caring and respect for his listeners as a writer should show for his readers is not to praise the tame and the irresolute. It is to assert, however, that boldness and resolve should serve to expand minds and hearts and imagination and not to construct barriers of gratuitously offensive modes of expression over which students must leap before struggling with concepts. Style should open gates to learning, not lock them.

While an instructor's choice of methodology is certainly relevant to the question of academic freedom, and while methodology is an important element of an instructor's style, there is no question in this case of deliberately using an offensive technique in order to accomplish some rarefied purpose. Furthermore, even if a pedagogical method were involved, a student's rights to study in a climate free of intimidation and in an environment that is nondemeaning would supersede the instructor's right to choose a method of instruction that intimidates and demeans.

If a discussion of the above with Dr. Frame leads to an understanding that the use of inappropriate levels of language in instruction may demean the students and trivialize the subject matter; if she comes to see that even if such language may on occasion bring the topic "home," "home" is precisely where one should not be, then, you might simply seek a promise that the lady change her style. After all, she is young and inexperienced and given to seeking *haute couture* rather than *prêt-à-porter*.

You should not, under any circumstance, follow the advice of the Affirmative Action officer and ask the chair to monitor her examinations. Any faculty member, albeit young and nontenured, who needs that close a supervision should be dismissed. It is one thing to advise, quite another to guard. Nor should you undermine her position by asking her to apologize. At best her mistake was motivated by a naive definition of honesty; at worst by a desire to rouse the bourgeoisie. Nor should you accept as any kind of a solution her proposed jejune consumer label tacked to her syllabus. No student should have to submit to such conditions in order to take a course.

You are, of course, dealing with a flamboyant type. The fire in her might make her into a superb teacher, but, then, she may not be able to bank the flames. If a discussion with her does not lead to agreement and reform, write her a formal letter of reprimand in which you make clear the institution's position and the consequences of running counter to it. Should the same charges be repeated and substantiated in a subsequent semester, terminate her contract. The cost of studying anthropology should not include the violation of a student's right to learn in a climate free of mental baiting.

No topic of discourse appropriate to the academy should be vulgarized by inappropriate language.

CHAPTER SIXTEEN
MANY ARE CALLED, FEW ARE CHOSEN
A CASE OF PART-TIME FACULTY

With each passing year, the young eighteenth-century divine pleased to be teaching a course in Greek while waiting to be assigned full-time ministerial duties grows increasingly quaint. He bears about the same resemblance to the contemporary part-time faculty member as does the colonial soap maker to Esteé Lauder. The analogy limps, as most analogies do, in one respect: The life of academe's contemporary transient is devoid of glamour. He is more likely to teach remedial English than Greek and he is unlikely to be waiting to be called by God or any of His emissaries. Instead of strolling across the yard reciting lines from Aeschylus, he runs to catch a subway in hopes of reaching an office, which he shares with four fellow-travelers, before the department secretary locks the duplicating room. Instead of discussing the meaning of Odysseus's wanderings, he justifiably worries about his own.

The part-time faculty taxonomy is widely known.

1. The Hopeful: A Ph.D. who longs to be considered for the next full-time opening or an A.B.D. who is probably taking his degree at a nearby research university. Both attempt to maintain self-esteem and dignity by viewing their condition as temporary.

2. The Independent: A person engaged in full-time nonacademic work (say in an accounting firm, a real-estate firm, an R&D arm of a high-technology company) who teaches a class for money and/or pleasure and/or perceived prestige.

3. The Self-Impeded: A person who has defined a chosen life-style as incompatible with full-time employment, for example, a mother of preschool children, an artist who hoards time for his canvases, etc.

4. The Attached: A retired professor who has not yet had enough of apple picking.

5. The Mysterious: A person who feels unobliged to give an account of himself. Rumors have it that he's writing a novel, cutting coupons from municipal bonds, perfecting a portable micro in his garage, hiding from three previous wives in as many states.

On any campus, this track team will include both long-distance runners and sprinters; some will teach year after year and become dedicated members of an academic community, while others will be there one semester and be gone forever the next. In addition, no classification can be rigid, for part-timers will cross from one category to the next and even, on occasion, keep a foot in two simultaneously. A Hopeful may also be a Self-Impeded, an Independent, a Hopeful, and all to various degrees will surely be Mysterious. Any categorizing is useful only to the extent that it identifies an individual's central attractions to part-time teaching and the same individual's central obstacle to his obtaining a full-time position. For such knowledge is essential in making decisions which affect part-time faculty.

What is far less well known than the taxonomy, however, are the solutions to the many problems that have glued themselves to the employment of part-time faculty as barnacles to the hull of a ship. Several relate to an institution's quality control: What policies should be established and what practices should be followed in the orientation and evaluation of part-time faculty? How does one determine the number of part-time faculty appropriate for a particular college/university? Is it wise to assign part-time faculty to a large number of an institution's introductory courses? Other questions, equally complex and equally controversial, focus on fair play: Do colleges/universities exploit part-time faculty? If so, do economic and social conditions justify such exploitation? Should the principles governing the marketplace also govern higher education? Is the issue a simple one of supply and demand?

THE BACKGROUND

You are midway through your second year in office as chief academic officer of a large urban nonunionized comprehensive university in the North. Your predecessor had cultivated an image of a gentle, kind pater familias who found it impossible to deny his children. Even the beneficiaries of such self-indulgence admitted, albeit with lowered voices, that the old man should often have said no when he had said yes. But he had held this position for 14 years and had been a member of the history department 20 years before that. To seek his ouster was as unthinkable as blowing up the campanile.

Furthermore, with lowered eyes and pious voice, he would announce once a year, usually with the quad decorated for commencement as background, that the next was very likely his last. He then took great pleasure in changing his mind and watching everyone mask disappointment. He was, in a word, as manipulative as anyone consciously dedicated to mild manners.

By applying his quite adequate intellect to the task, he had perfected the art of avoiding. He knew where the university's cracks were, but he was not one by temperament to swing on scaffolds and in the last few years age had allowed him to avoid heights without the inconvenience of self-reproach. He also knew that cracks need time to widen; these walls were not apt to crumble on anyone but his successor. And if the latter had to dodge a few stones, better to be young in the worst of times than old in the best of times. He remembered Robert Lowell saying that. The thought had served him well for years.

The faculty had, perhaps unconsciously, sought both retribution and relief by recommending you as his replacement. The two of you had neither personally nor professionally one trait in common, and they had made it clear that deferred maintenance was no longer acceptable.

You have spent your first 6 months taking a careful inventory of the university's most pressing needs and, then, set about in a systematic fashion to address one after the other. Since academics have rarely been accused of speeding, you are still after a year and a half well at the top of your long priority list. Among the dragons left to slay is a possibly large dangerous one described innocently as: "Apparent excessive and unfair (?) and unwise (?) use of part-time faculty."

THE HAPPENING

It is the week before Christmas and all through the university faculty, students, and staff are gathering around festive-colored punch bowls. While there are end-of-term examinations to take and to grade, even the duplicating machine sports a cheerful sprig of holly and you have received as a welcomed gift time for your own self-examination. Since you now know the campus far better than you had a year ago, should you reorder your priorities? Should you attempt to deal with several more items on the list simultaneously? The university senate has already doubled its meeting time this fall semester. Are you asking too much of the faculty? Your mind swings leisurely and pleasantly between these questions and the Handel tape serving as an accompaniment to thought. You decide that even an oratorio can effectively carry only an appropriate number of themes, and you return your list to your desk drawer. A sensible decision perhaps in all respects but one: Not only do we all march to different drummers, we all keep our own calendars. We alone hear the first and see the second. Events are about to remind you that you should never expect others to divine either the music you hear or the rhythm you keep.

Two days before the end of the term, two part-time members of the faculty, a Hopeful and a Self-Impeded, ask to see you. It is clear from the outset of the meeting that neither has been unduly influenced by Christmas cheer. Indeed, the season's call for happiness has undoubtedly exacerbated what they view as their unjust plight. H., a man in his early thirties who holds a Ph.D. in European philosophy from a reputable research university, has never been offered a permanent position but once: in a small denominational college in a rural area remote from theaters and concert halls, which are not only important but essential to him. S-I., a woman in her late twenties and a mother of two preschoolers, had abandoned half completed doctoral studies when her husband's career took him from the East to the West Coast. She is a graduate of one of the seven-sisters from which college she also received an M.A. in sociology. Both are intelligent, articulate, well-mannered, and very angry. Beneath the anger swims a depression that surfaces frequently enough to engage much of your attention.

You must understand that the situation is simply intolerable. After 4 years at this university they are still treated as untouchables. The pay alone, about $1,100 a course, spells exploitation, but consider that the pay is the whole of the compensation received by a part-time member of your faculty. There are no fringe benefits of any kind: no medical and dental insurance, no faculty development funds, no assurance from one semester of employment to the next, no parking privileges, no decent office space, no adequate secretarial help. In a word, they work without dignity.

And the lack of respect with which the university treats them is underscored in most departments including their own by their exclusion from faculty meetings and from all collegial decision making in matters of curriculum and standards. If the chair of a department finds 30 unruly freshmen in Room 210 of Old Main and no one behind the lectern, he pulls in a part-timer from the streets. If the noise in Room 210 subsides, the part-timer is given a temporary library card, and if he is lucky, someone points him in the direction of that library. If peace does not reign or students complain about the nature of it, the part-timer is unceremoniously returned to the streets and the chair issues a temporary library card to another itinerant who leans on the lectern with feigned nonchalance and confidence. In your view, does this conveyor belt mentality reflect the values of academe? Should it? Is it to enter this world that one reads Spinoza and Durkheim into the night?

Once you confess that the conditions as described most assuredly do not reflect your values nor those of a caring academy, H. and S-I.'s anger subsides and their puzzlement rises. If such be the case, why have you not addressed the issue? No one had any hope that your predecessor would, but after a year and a half neither have you. True, they recognize that you have devoted long hours to curriculum development, especially the general university requirements, and you have made clear as had never been done before the criteria for promotion and tenure. But had you concluded that the welfare of faculty who teach as many as 35% of the students in some departments was of little importance? Since to their knowledge you have never mentioned the part-time faculty in any of your memos or your addresses to the faculty, many have surmised that your head and your heart were elsewhere.

Consequently, a significant number of part-time faculty have been meeting informally in small groups and the tension at these meetings registers above the danger mark. H. and S-I. have taken it upon themselves to attempt some constructive action. They hand you a written statement signed by 96 part-time faculty, which summarizes their grievances and requests that you meet with them at an open forum immediately after the holidays.

Your protestations and explanations strike even you as somewhat lame. Good intentions are a thin blanket against the cold. You set a date for the meeting and you part wishing one another a happy holiday.

You have long since understood that no administrator should ever enter a meeting uninformed and/or unequipped. If this rule is ever broken, it most certainly should never be when meeting with a group small or large that seeks redress to perceived injustices. There is the immediate preparation consisting of the gathering of pertinent facts and data, of studying the history of the complaint, of understanding the cultural and emotional context of the upheaval. Of equal importance is the bringing to bear on the issue in a clearly articulated manner the values and principles accumulated through years of study and experience. Just as a scientist will spend half a lifetime honing his mind to recognize a discovery when it occurs, so too an academic administrator should have a depth of intellectual resources upon which to draw at the drop of a gavel. When someone yells "Fire" is not the time to read about the proper methods of putting it out.

However, in this case, you have been hit hard on your blind side. The university's Office of Institutional Research, casual at best, has virtually no information on part-time faculty beyond the number of sections assigned to them in each department. Central Administration has no idea who they are or how well they do. Presumably, the chairs of the departments know something of their provenance and their performance, but they are trimming Christmas trees or packing for Key West or the Bahamas. You accept the fact that even the chairs' files, given the campus culture, are likely to provide patchy data and that patchy data, like a little learning, can be a dangerous thing. Hence, you prepare for the event by reading broadly on the use of part-time faculty in colleges/universities, by making sure that you understand all of the complexities associated with the practice, and by arriving at some preliminary conclusions regarding a system of justice that might answer some of the needs of both the institution and the part-time faculty. You have no intention, of course, of prematurely unveiling the last. You simply need it as a mental draft against which other proposals may be weighed.

The meeting attended by nearly a hundred part-time faculty members and chaired by H. takes place as scheduled. You had decided, wisely as it turned out, not to impose any restrictions on the discussion nor to insist upon a special format. This openness sets a proper climate for an honest exchange of views. The session is typically even stereotypically academic: Every view is exhaustively analyzed three times in increasingly polysyllabic terms. However, once the rhetoric clears, you face an exasperated, angry, and disillusioned group whose tone attributes ill will to anyone who makes decisions that affect them and whose anecdotal testimony is clearly sincere though at times myopic.

"I've been here 6 years and I know one thing. Administrators in this university have always treated full-time faculty members as colleagues. But where we're concerned, deans wear miters."

"It's the small indignities that get beneath my skin. I work in a department that will not allow part-time faculty access to the supply room. Maybe the department is right. With what it pays me I might well be tempted to sell its pencils on street corners."

"I've taught here for six consecutive semesters and the chair of my department is very friendly. He always greets me with a smile and a hearty 'Good morning, Ralph.' There's only one thing wrong. My name is Bruce."

"It's as if this place lacked the imagination to envision the need for order in the lives of people who are not full professors of semiotics. I never know from semester to semester whether I can count on teaching one section, or two sections, or no sections. At times I'm called on the very day classes begin."

"That's right. And it's not simply a question of order in your own life, but order in the classroom. Under these conditions, how can one prepare classes? Let alone find a proper day-care center that allows late registration and pick up another course at another school that treats you every bit as well."

"I'll tell you what is most depressing about my life in this institution of supposedly higher learning. I've had a Ph.D. in English for 2 years now and I sit here with two friends who have had theirs even longer than I have. All three of us care passionately about our field and every other day we walk into a department where 50% of the tenured faculty give no evidence of caring about it at all. Semester after semester they sing their mockingbird songs when they bother to sing at all and we're not even given an audition. Try that one for stress."

"Can you name another group in this country with 18 to 22 years of schooling that often can't afford medical insurance?"

"As a full-time faculty member, I was involved in many of the decisions on this campus. Now that I've retired and teach but one course a semester I'm treated as if I'd undergone a lobotomy."

"Look, after all is said and nothing done, it comes to this: Are the values of this university identical to those of an insti-

tution whose mission is profit? If they are, then put an end to
the high-minded discourses, the inspiring commencement addresses, the lovely ideals in the front of the catalogue and frankly
announce that you're taking the low road. That way this place
will distinguish itself by supporting one academic standard of
excellence: honesty."

"With all due respect, in the academy 'administrator' has
become a euphemism for 'accountant.' If we admit that, we can
all go home."

On it goes. Surely there is enough force in both the substance
and style of the accusations and criticisms to open the sluices of
your own self-pity. In an Ibsen drama you might walk out and
slam the door behind you, but the trouble with walking out in
that fashion is the difficulty of returning with any degree of grace.
You brush aside the temptation and adopt a tone that leans neither
to servility nor to authority. At the bottom of the list of what the
university's part-time faculty need at this juncture is a weak administrator who is intimidated by their anger and in some instances their self-righteousness. And the next to the last is to be
reminded that they are at the mercy of your power. Though their
grievances may have merit, your values are not those of the
sweatshop and you do not allow a crowd to persuade you that
they are. By taking no remark personally, by addressing the issues
calmly and kindly, by firmly refusing to be stampeded into making
promises that you might not be able to keep, you convince the
group that the orderly way of approaching the issues raised is to
establish an ad hoc committee of the university senate to conduct
a study and to recommend solutions to whatever problems exist.
You detect the predictable snickering to what some undoubtedly
view as a bureaucratic substitute for decisive action. However,
you persist in following that route for two reasons: one, you need
time for the gathering and analysis of data and information, and,
two, you cannot without potentially serious consequences make
unilateral decisions regarding matters that will, at least in some
instances, significantly affect the full-time faculty. You assure
everyone that a proportionately appropriate number of part-time
faculty will sit on the proposed committee and that you are sympathetic to their plight. At the end of the 2-hour session, the tension in the room has perceptibly diminished.

With the concurrence and help of the Executive Committee
of the university senate you establish the Committee on Part-Time
Faculty Status and charge it to report to the senate at its last meet-

ing of the academic year in mid-May. The committee is made up of four full-time faculty members, two part-time faculty members, and your assistant vice-president who sits as a nonvoting member and who is to keep you informed as to the directions taken and progress made throughout the next few months.

On the agreed-upon date the ad hoc committee, chaired by a conscientious, peace-loving, and sympathetic historian, presents the senate with a reasonably thorough report that includes relevant data based upon a study of the actual working conditions of the university's part-time faculty, perceptions of these conditions derived from a questionnaire sent to all part-time faculty members (73% response rate), the results of interviews with department chairs and of open hearings with the full-time faculty, and certain circumstances of the professional lives of the university's part-time faculty recommended for further study and possible change.

First, the facts.

Part-time FTE faculty and number of sections taught by part-time faculty in the current academic year shows a slight increase from the previous 5 years, but the figures have been fairly stable during that length of time since enrollment has remained level. Your full-time faculty carry a 12-hour teaching load.

Part-time FTEF		Number of Sections	% of all Sections
Arts and Sciences:			
Biology	2.50	10	11.24
Chemistry	1.75	7	13.21
Computer science	1.00	4	4.08
English	13.50	54	27.00
Geography	2.00	8	17.02
History	0.75	3	3.33
Mathematics	9.25	37	25.52
Modern languages	3.50	14	24.14
Philosophy	2.25	9	18.37
Physics	1.75	7	10.77
Political science	1.00	4	9.09
Psychology	13.00	52	27.51
Sociology	2.00	8	8.00
Business and Economics:			
Accounting & Finance	5.25	21	23.33
Business (Management & Marketing)	13.75	55	25.11
Economics	2.75	11	15.71

Part-time FTEF		Number of Sections	% of all Sections
Education:			
Early childhood	0.50	2	5.71
Elementary	0.50	2	9.52
Secondary	0.25	1	2.86
Fine Arts:			
Art	3.25	13	8.44
Dance	3.00	12	38.71
Mass communication	9.75	39	25.83
Music	3.25	13	5.04
Theater arts	4.25	17	29.31
Health and Physical Education:			
Health			
Nursing	3.25	13	27.08
Occupational therapy	0.50	2	6.06
Physical education	2.25	9	5.06
Speech pathology and audiology	8.00	32	51.61

Additional pertinent information on the university's part-time faculty:

59% are male.

57% teach one course; 25% teach two courses; 18% teach three courses.

13% are in their first year with the university; 12% are in their second; 21% are in their third; 54% have been teaching at the university for 4 years or more.

84%, hired at the rank of instructor, are paid at the low end of a scale that reads:

Instructor—$1,050 per course
Assistant professor—$1,150 per course
Associate professor—$1,300 per course
Professor—$1,400 per course

21% are Hopefuls; 33% are Independents; 36% are Self-Impeded; 2% are Attached; 8% are Mysterious.

18% have not been provided with office space but all are expected to confer with students when requested.

51% are without health benefits from any employer.

55% are not invited to attend departmental meetings.

54% did not receive an orientation to the university during their first semester on campus.

The questionnaire distributed to the part-time faculty revealed the following concerns in order of priority.

1. Inadequate salary
2. Isolation from full-time faculty members
3. Alienation from the university's mission
4. Lack of involvement in policy decisions that affect them
5. Lack of respect
6. Lack of job security
7. Lack of office space
8. Lack of fringe benefits

The interviews with the chairs uncovered a cleavage between those who in support of the demands of the part-time faculty had already tried to meet some of them and those who beneath a more or less heavy patina of rhetoric hid a conviction that in an ideal academic setting one would not need part-timers to protect the real faculty from the vicissitudes occasioned by inadequate budgets and from the indignity of teaching illiterate freshmen.

The open hearings to which all full-time faculty had been invited had been very poorly attended. However, the few who had come had expressed disapproval of raising part-time faculty salaries until the salaries of full-time faculty had been raised to an acceptable level; of guaranteeing employment to part-timers until guarantees had been given to every full-time faculty member who wanted to teach an overload; and of allowing faculty who are here one semester and elsewhere the next to have a say in policies that affect those who are permanent members of the institution.

Perhaps cowed and restrained by those chairs and the few full-time faculty members who were hostile to its aims or perhaps convinced that the hostility could be reduced by mildness, the committee makes its recommendations in the most tentative of manners. As a result, and at the very last minute and to the chagrin of the chair, the two members of the committee who represented the part-time faculty pin to that portion of the report a minority view that, in effect, objects to what they judge to be a pusillanimous tone symptomatic of the university's false values. They do, however, agree with the substance of the recommendations.

In a voice somewhat akin to that of a novice addressing his abbot, the report suggests that the university might consider studying the feasibility of improving the lot of part-time faculty by:

1. Raising salaries
2. Providing health insurance
3. Providing sick leave
4. Instituting a tuition waiver plan
5. Guaranteeing greater job security and timely notification of employment
6. Encouraging incorporation into the faculty evaluation and merit pay system
7. Allowing representation on the university senate
8. Establishing uniform orientation procedures
9. Permitting attendance at departmental meetings

The report is distributed a week before the scheduled senate meeting as that body's constitution demands. Rumors abound. In accordance with the emotional propensities of the narrator rather than with an evaluation of the facts, the part-time faculty are disappointed or distressed or angry or outraged by the jelly firmness of the recommendations. Depending on conclusions drawn from a conversation with two colleagues in the hallway between classes rather than on a reliable survey, the full-time faculty are worried or distressed or angry or outraged by outsiders who seek the privileges of insiders. Only one thing seems certain: Those who slept are now awake.

The meeting hall is crowded with many who a week ago could not have told you in what building the university senate held its monthly sessions. You suppress a smile as you scan the room, for its occupants represent academe's version of the cliché casting of World War II films where a Jew from the Bronx, an Italian Catholic from California, a blond farmhand from Minnesota, and a Mexican American from Santa Fe got the better of the Japanese in Burma. Waiting patiently while the errors to the minutes of the last meeting are pointed out with grave precision and some pleasure are the Feminists in Guatemalan shawls here perhaps to protect the rights of their sisters; the Elders pale in chalk-sprinkled outmoded suits here perhaps to guard the doctrine that a university *is* its full-time faculty; the junior faculty in fashionable oversized sweaters here perhaps in support of the first half of a Spanish proverb that claims that if you are not a rebel in youth, you have no heart and if you are one in age, you have no head. Ah, well, it is spring.

While in class B films stereotypes can be expected to behave in stereotypical ways, to predict endings in the academic constitutes an adventure, for in this world even the unoriginal think. The members of the senate yield time after time to members of the audience who ask to speak and the meeting becomes progressively noisy and polemical. Those in attendance seem to be evenly divided, according to no perceptible line of age, rank, or conditions of appointment, between those who would right an injustice to part-time faculty who should be treated as colleagues and those who quite bluntly assert that attempts to extend the privileges of a community of scholars to those who in many instances could not meet its criteria would be to weaken the university. In the latter's view, no one is forced to accept part-time employment and the university has never misrepresented the compensation offered in return for services rendered. To raise salaries by a modest amount and to offer some fringe benefits one might accept, providing the university could fund such an increase without decreasing the support of other equally worthy demands, but long-term guarantees and full participation in policymaking are not in the nature of part-time association in any institution whether it be a university or a business firm. Understandably, neither the part-time faculty nor their sympathizers are willing to accept such a system of metaphysics and eagerly describe their version of the "nature" of part-time association.

After 2 hours of inconclusive debate, the senate, perhaps convinced that all relevant arguments have been heard at least twice, perhaps inspired by the call of the end-of-term papers that blanket both their desks and their chairs, defeat first a motion to table until the September meeting and, then, a motion to recess, in order to call for the question.

All those in favor of accepting the "Report of the Committee on the Status of Part-time Faculty" with the understanding that the administration study the feasibility of implementing its recommendations raise your hand:

Those in favor—15

Those opposed—15

The chair then invokes her privilege to break a tie and votes in favor. The meeting is adjourned, and the room is charged with peevish remarks. Each player would like to believe that his backhand is far more impressive than this match displayed and goes home to replay the games so that his strokes may shine before storage in his memory.

SUGGESTED COURSE OF ACTION

In a predicament such as this one, the two options you do not want to exercise are hesitancy or flight. Dive through the wave, for otherwise you will find yourself wondering how to dispose of a mouthful of sand. Unlike your predecessor, you are no university monument.

What the senate did in effect was to tell you to find a solution to a problem that it could not resolve. Though the vote cast by the chair resulted in a call for an investigation of the possibility of improving the lot of part-time faculty, such a timid resolution might more appropriately be considered a whispered request than a summon to action. Conceivably, therefore, you could survive politically and even attract supporters among the full-time faculty by playing out the clock. You could study each subissue in a leisurely fashion and occasionally distribute a palliative. If adept at this type of manipulative game, you might not rouse to action any of the combatants for years. Everyone might even go back to sleep. After all, the heat of the summer has been known to melt many a spring resolve, and, besides, the most aggressive and least satisfied part-time faculty are the very ones likely to leave the institution.

However, such hesitancy and such avoidance is unacceptable administrative behavior for at least two serious reasons. One, it is dishonest. After only 6 months in your position you had decided that the use and status of part-time faculty was an issue that had to be addressed. The only thing this tempest has done is blown your calendar about and allowed you to gauge the force of the opposing winds, which is possibly heavier than you had assumed. Two, an administrator is known by the values he keeps. The first operative question here as elsewhere is "What is right?" not "What is expedient?" and the second is "How much of the right is it possible to bring about?" not "How much effort will this right

cost?" Here is a grand opportunity for you to set a tone for your administration by persuading the academic community to ask the right questions and to seek generous answers.

However, while you do not want to avoid the issue, you do want to avoid the many dangers that accompany it.

Danger #1: You assume that because the university senate has in effect told you to seek a disposition to the problem, the faculty will accept any solution, however elegant, which you in solitary splendor declare to be just. As soon as possible, meet with the chair of the senate and establish a task force charged with helping you to find ways to implement as many of the ad hoc committee's recommendations as the short- and long-term good of the university will allow. In this case, the chair of the senate has three very important attributes: one, presumably she has the respect and confidence of the faculty; two, since she cast the decisive affirmative vote, she is sympathetic to seeking justice for the part-time faculty; and, three, she is courageous. Her vote saved you from a dilemma far worse than the one you now confront, namely, accepting the status quo or vetoing a senate resolution. All views should be represented on this task force and it should continue working on its charge until you consider it fulfilled. To indicate your strong commitment to the aims of this task force's efforts, you might periodically issue progress reports via memos to the faculty and/or updates to the university senate.

Danger #2: You assume that the few full-time faculty members who have made their views known at hearings held by the ad hoc committee or at the May meeting of the university senate speak for the entire or even the majority of the faculty. There may well be hundreds of faculty out there studying the mating habits of salamanders or the use of violent imagery in Flannery O'Connor who would be receptive to improving the professional standing of part-time faculty colleagues as long as you do not disturb them on Tuesdays when they write. All faculty must be made aware of the issue, the problems that attend it, and the values that the university hopes to promote in preferring certain solutions to others.

Danger #3: Your rhetoric becomes self-righteous and reproachful of those who quite openly place their own welfare and comfort above the minimum needs of others. You must be very careful to cultivate a persuasive tone that does not place those who oppose part-time faculty as colleagues into a position where they must defend their lack of appetite for sacrifice and from which there is no graceful exit. For doing so could worsen the condition of part-time faculty in some departments by transforming innocent phantoms into vampires. You might thus even disrupt the harmony that already exists in some departments.

Danger #4: Your goodwill is viewed as precipitating actions and the formulation of policies that are not synchronized with the long-range plans of the university. "Justice above all ledgers" reverberates nicely in any hall regardless of acoustics, but issues are rarely reduced to such simplicities. Here, for instance, the first question the task force should address is not even among the ad hoc committee's recommendations. Before coming to some conclusion regarding salaries and office space and all other sources of displeasure, the university should determine what portion of its faculty should be employed part time. Some of its departments, for example, business, mathematics, speech pathology, psychology, would be judged by most criteria as set forth by accrediting and evaluation agencies to be unacceptably high. Once guidelines governing the number of part-time faculty to be employed in each department, depending on its individual needs, have been established and incorporated into the long-range plans of the university, then and only then should the responsibilities and privileges of those hired be established.

A fair and just and respectful treatment of part-time faculty, like fairness and justice and respect in nearly all instances, cannot be determined in the abstract. Those judged to be below the poverty level in one country might be referred to as middle class in another. Likewise, a proper salary and appropriate fringe benefits in one university could be rank exploitation in another. Only a thorough study of the university's budget will allow any task force to draw conclusions. The question of an equitable share of office space will also depend upon an analysis of space utilization. If two university senior professors share an office originally designed for one, two first-year part-time faculty might not unfairly be asked to share a desk.

However, even those universities who cope with roller-coaster budgets and inadequate space can and should establish dignified working conditions that take into account the professional nature of the part-time faculty members' obligations. After arriving at specific recommendations regarding their salary, fringe benefits, and office space, the task force you have established should formulate policies governing their precise and appropriate role in university and departmental governance particularly as regards curricula and standards, their proper orientation and evaluation, and their just and timely notification of assignment from year to year.

None of these policies should be taken to the university senate for approval until departmental chairs and a majority of the full-time faculty have agreed to support them. The target you have in sight, inclusion of the part-time faculty into the university's community of scholars, will grow considerably larger and may even stop moving if your task force distinguishes between continuing part-time faculty who most probably teach more than one course per term and those who teach but an occasional course or who disappear after 1 year. Consensus is also more likely to be reached if your task force makes clear the expectations that accompany the privileges. In addition, in order to boost everyone's sense of progress, you should not wait for total agreement on every subtopic before returning to the senate. Confirmation of the whole will eventually be achieved if your task force gets part after part ratified. This partitioned approach will be effective as long as everyone understands the values that are operative and as long as these values are consistently applied.

In sum, while some full-time faculty feel economically and/ or politically threatened by part-time faculty, universities need them for program flexibility and staff enrichment and, hence, will continue to employ them. Unless one refuses to accept this premise, the only serious question deals with determining a part-time faculty member's responsibilities and privileges. It simply will not do for nonresearch universities to boast that none of their classes are conducted by teaching assistants when as many as a third of their courses are taught by questionably qualified and unsupervised faculty who are pulled from kitchens and garrets and real-estate firms the week before the opening of a term. Many a college/ university student's introduction to a discipline is assigned to a part-time faculty member; many a freshman's initiation to the academic world is conducted by a part-time faculty member. Hence, institutions that allow this practice owe these instructors the respect of colleagues. And respect in academe means both support and evaluation. To withhold either is to admit through negligence that teaching can be entrusted to nearly anyone humble or desperate enough to do it under virtually any demeaning condition.

A college/university that tolerates such negligence drastically diminishes its credibility.

The deferred maintenance of faculty, both full time and part time, is more dangerous and serious a matter than the deferred maintenance of buildings and grounds.

CHAPTER SEVENTEEN
BORN AND MADE

Once upon a time there lived a provost and seven deans. All eight worked in a university where goodwill reigned. One dark and drizzly January day, the severely understaffed Office of Admissions, further handicapped by a breakdown of its mainframe computer, was attacked by anxiety. Thousands of application forms and assorted informational booklets were to have been mailed weeks ago. If prospective students did not receive these forms and brochures very soon, they would most probably be late in applying for financial aid and might choose to attend a rival university that had been prompt in responding to requests or, worst yet, might decide not to go to college at all.

The provost decided to solve the immediate problem by throwing a "Backlog Party" to which all seven deans were invited. Between 5:00 p.m. and 10:00 p.m., with a 30-minute break for pizza and coke, one midweek evening the eight upper level administrators and the Admissions Office staff labeled and stuffed envelopes, updated files, and prepared bulk-mailing pouches. Office clerks delighted in giving directions to executives and the latter exaggerated their need for instruction to the general entertainment of everyone. The party was a huge success.

The most amusing events connected with this affair, however, were the spontaneous responses of each of the deans who received his invitation from the provost by telephone.

DEAN 1: "A party? Terrific. Where and at what time?"

DEAN 2: "I'll be happy to help, but, tell me, why is this necessary? I mean just this morning I read the weekly Admissions Statistical Report and the number of applications and contracts received is almost exactly the same as it was last year at this time. They weren't worried about keeping up then. At least I didn't hear about it and we met our projections."

DEAN 3: "O.K. I'll come, but Admissions owes us."

DEAN 4: "I'll be there. But, listen, are you sure you haven't been reading too many Japanese management books? I'm going to send you a good biography of Louis XIV just for a change of pace."

DEAN 5: "I'm with you as long as I get pizza with double anchovies and a glass of Chianti Classico."

DEAN 6: "Gee, I don't know. I would certainly like to help out. Don't misunderstand. I think it's a great idea, but my wife's mother (I guess that makes her my mother-in-law doesn't it—ha!) has a brother who just had a stroke and we're taking care of his dog who's so lonely he won't eat and my wife who's been bearing the brunt of all this sprained her ankle running after the dog and she has a PTA meeting that night. But, listen, it's a super gesture and I'm going to do my very best to be there."

DEAN 7: "That does it. This is the third week in a row that I miss the Bill Cosby Show. I'm buying a VCR and charging it to the university. I'm watching so little T.V. that my mind is turning to mush. Count me in. I'm ready to stuff envelopes."

Now in this little parable, if you play the part of the provost, undoubtedly, some of the responses will please you more than others. However, if you decide that some of the responses are better than others in an absolute sense, or that there was among them one and only one proper academic administrator's voice, you may wish to pause and to consider whether, indeed, such is the case.

Academic administration that is not limited to managerial tasks and bureaucratic duties provides leadership for a community of persons who are among the most knowledgeable, the most talented, the most curious, and the most independent in the world. To be persuasive and effective in that context is a demanding art form and an artist should be allowed his signature. Indeed, an artist whose style is not distinguishably his own is by that very fact alone often consigned to mediocrity. Matisse's blue is a shade of blue that belongs to no one but Matisse. Likewise a successful administrator's every decision, every response, every plan, every paper, and every talk bears the bold imprint of his quality of mind and heart as opposed to the faint and nondistinctive seal of a mimetic personality.

Even in the above responses, admittedly too short and dealing with too unimportant an issue to lead to anything but possibly entertaining conclusions, a personality that is not cautious in re-

vealing itself comes forth, as well it should. If universities are institutions dedicated in part to youth's discovery and formulation
of self and analysis of other selves, then it will not do to be satisfied
with leaders who are interchangeable. The difference between an
administrator whose voice can be easily recognized and one who
mimics that of others is the difference between receiving a love
letter written by someone who loves baseball and plays the flute
and one copied from a manual of 101 samples.

Anyone who has ever sat on committees searching for a dean
or vice-president who surpasses all deans or all vice-presidents
will have learned after long hours of interviewing that standards
of perfection and excellence are but infrequently what distinguishes one potential administrator from another. When was the
last time you heard anyone describe his administrative style as
dictatorial? Every candidate in line for anointment professes belief
in academic freedom, integrity in intercollegiate sports, the importance of collegiality and clean windowpanes. Furthermore, all
of the finalists will have called meetings to order, chaired committees, cut the mustard, made the tough decisions, bitten the
bullet, fished or cut bait, and thrown the hard ball. But not all of
them when sitting with others at a round table will have defined
its head. Those who have will lead; the others will manage, perhaps even well.

Hence, you improve your own vision by wearing bifocals and
seek fellow administrators who wear them also. Up close, you do
not develop a self, a style, a voice, from a kit, a how-to-manual,
a simplistic list of steps, an artificial and superimposed set of
manners. At a distance, you neither attempt to impose conformity
nor give unanimity more than its due. In *Glory* Vladimir Nabokov
says of an old Russian emigre who falls prone on the sidewalk,
dead of heart failure, that the "obituary writer's words 'he burned
with love for Russia' or 'he always held high his pen' somehow
debased the deceased . . ." since these same words would have
been equally applicable to others. What was truly irreplaceable
was the originality of the deceased: ". . . his gestures, his beard,
his sculpturesque wrinkles, the sudden shy smile, the jacket but-
ton that hung by a thread, and his way of licking a stamp with
his entire tongue before sticking it on the envelope and banging
it with his fist" (McGraw-Hill, New York, 1971, pp. 142–143).

Obviously, no one would advocate choosing an administrator
on the basis of how he licks a stamp, but the Nabokov passage
is a beautiful and touching metaphorical insight illustrative of the

first criterion for academic administrative leadership: a personality that is neither primarily mimetic nor overly attracted by simplicity and conformity. When you knock, there is someone home.

However, being there and having a distinguishable voice with which to answer is only the beginning. The tenor Placido Domingo is not asked to sing the role of a bass or a baritone. Are there qualities that always characterize an effective, a successful administrative voice in the academy? It would be difficult to argue that one could lead without inspiring trust and it would be nearly impossible to inspire trust without being scrupulously truthful. And it would be equally difficult to predict a long and honorable career for someone who, in imitation of the American military officer in 1945 who looked at the ancient Roman ruins and said, "We sure did a thorough job of that," could never share kudos with anyone, not even Father Time. (This anecdote forms part of Natalia Danest Murray's commentary on the letters of Janet Flanner in *Darlinghissima: Letters to A Friend*, Random House, New York, 1985, p. 19.) But aside from integrity and generosity, and at least a modicum of humility, virtues that are to be cultivated in any enterprise, are there other qualities essential to the life of an academic administrator?

Though few convictions can lead healthy lives without qualifications, significant accomplishments are highly unlikely for those academic administrators who have not mastered language and who have not developed broad intellectual interests.

Let us for a moment fantasize. Every now and then one reads an interview that runs along this track:

INTERVIEWER: Dr. Badenheim, would you tell our listeners when and how you became interested in astrophysics.

DR. BADENHEIM: When I was 4, my father, who worked in the coal mines of West Virginia, gave me a *History of The World* for Christmas and I became fascinated with the idea that the world had not always been here and this led to an interest in the concept of infinity. By the age of 9 I was grinding my own telescopic lenses and 4 years later designing computer graphics to illustrate the laws that account for the behavior of matter and energy.

INTERVIEWER: I see.

Now imagine an academic administrator responding to an interviewer on a parallel track:

INTERVIEWER: Dr. Hudson, would you tell our listeners when and how you became interested in academic administration.

DR. HUDSON: When I was 6 I was ill with pneumonia and kept out of school for 3 weeks. My father, who worked in a logging camp in Maine, brought home a book that he had found in a cave. It was called *In Search of The One Minute Manager*. I was immediately attracted to the concept of time/motion studies. The following year I reorganized my mother's kitchen to improve her productivity and the rest is history. I traveled from the discovery of one management tool to another until I arrived at academic administration where, as you know, I'm now developing tests to measure an administrator's integrity. Truth tests. It's the future.

That the first interview is parody and the second tomfoolery suggests that while certain careers, such as scientific research, may best be met head on, others, academic administration among them, are best approached obliquely. Some in the field who have experienced its demands gave a touching testimonial to that view in the July/August 1985 issue of *Change*. A majority of the professional journal's readers who were polled confessed that if they had it to do over again, they would major in English. Not in management, not in higher education, but in English. Why? After all, all of the liberal arts should lift one beyond the confines of one's limited and narrow perspectives. The mind's eye came to rest upon English because of all the disciplines this one has as its primary goal a mastery of language and because this one encourages a broad knowledge of allied disciplines necessary for a sensitive interpretation of texts. In a word, this discipline's direct ends coincide with the two qualifications identified above as indispensable to effective academic leadership: spirited, even memorable use of language, and intellectual curiosity that demonstrates a life of the mind not fenced in by immediate bureaucratic and/or political concerns. This is not to suggest that these qualities of mind may not be developed in a multitude of ways through a multitude of disciplines. It is, however, to point out that through the study of English one attempts perhaps in the most direct of ways to cultivate these qualities, and it is to insist, even at the expense of crankiness, that their importance to leadership in the academic can hardly be exaggerated.

No academic community will be inspired by an idea that is poorly expressed. Perhaps as confirmation of Pascal's adage that what is clearly understood is easily expressed, no one in the intellectual world will rise and follow the inarticulate. One has witnessed hostility tempered by the turn of a phrase, irrationality subdued by a beautifully balanced sentence, convictions wrenched by an arresting metaphor. And one has also seen difficult matters made worse, most often unconsciously, through the insensitive use of language. An anecdote that has gained credence on one campus, but which may have been created by a wag in search of illustration, traces the contempt of a professor for his dean to a 4-year-old note in which the latter wishing to praise the former thanked him for the "inordinate" amount of enthusiasm he had shown for a particular project.

Now to have a voice that is distinctive and to use it with style, with accuracy, and with grace are serious advantages only if an academic administrator has something to say that is worth hearing. While "that something to say" should obviously include thoughtful views regarding academe's perennial issues, for example, the curriculum that will outdistance all curricula, the standards that will support both quality and access; and academe's questions du jour, for example, bills pending before various legislative committees that would affect higher education, and resolutions being debated by national and state accrediting agencies, an academic administrator's life of the mind should never be limited to these concerns. A profession that by its very nature calls for an understanding of and a commitment to intellectuals in dozens of disciplines and requires decision making that often determines the growth or stagnation of scholarship in fields as diverse as theater arts and molecular biology should not trust its enlightenment solely to readings and workshops on NCAA skirmishes and student recruitment strategies.

However, if one were to judge the breadth and depth of the contemporary academic administrator's intellectual interests by scanning the topics discussed at professional conferences and by running down the table of contents of the publications of the proceedings one could only conclude that many are attracted by a soporific repetition and pleased by narrow channels as opposed to open seas. The contemporary British novelist David Lodge may be right: "The modern conference resembles the pilgrimage of medieval Christendom in that it allows the participants to indulge themselves in all the pleasures and diversions of travel while appearing to be austerely bent on self-improvement" (*Small World*, Macmillan, New York, 1984, Prologue).

When the profession decides to trade appearance for substance at its plenary sessions in the halls of the Hiltons and its concurrent sessions in the meeting rooms of the Sheratons it might begin by encouraging administrators to confine their narrowly bureaucratic concerns to satellite sessions and to invite as main speakers scholars who would brief those upon whom they depend for the support of their teaching and scholarship on the discoveries and directions and controversies of their disciplines. An academic administrator not trained as an anthropologist should nevertheless understand the questions surrounding the reliability and ethics of anthropological field notes; an academic administrator who is not a historian should nevertheless be aware of the controversy raging over scientific, value-free history; an academic administrator who is not a philosopher should nevertheless have a layman's knowledge of the arguments debated in the ethics of medicine, law, and agriculture. Not every academic administrator can be a psychologist or a chemist, but every academic administrator can be and should be aware of the work being done in behavioral toxicology and the importance of tools such as lasers and molecular beams for chemical research. An academic administrator must create conditions that encourage his institution's linguists to work with his neuropsychologists and biologists because theoretical advances in the nature of mental grammar is apt to come from interdisciplinary scholarship. There is no substitute for a broad knowledge of all the disciplines for wise decision making in academe. By comparison a knowledge of the sociological, political, and bureaucratic context in which learning in a college/university takes place year after year is small change. And while small change is useful, indeed necessary, it should never try to pass itself off as major currency.

One of the central ironies in the life-style of many an academic administrator is three-pronged. He will intone all the pious refrains in support of a liberal education as opposed to a narrow pre-professional training and, then, limit his own intellectual development to a knowledge of the most ephemeral and undemanding aspects of higher education: its daily operation. He will attack as hypocritical heads of firms whose rhetoric encourages students to engage in studies that expand the mind and then hire those who have concentrated on entry-level skills, and, then, choose as junior and midlevel administrators those who have prepared themselves only to understand flow charts and hegis codes and program evaluation systems. And, finally, he will denigrate legislators and members of advisory and regulatory boards for seeking the counsel of laymen as opposed to experts and, then, make decisions regarding a discipline with little if any knowledge of the major developments within that discipline. Consequently, he remains often at the mercy of his own ignorance or at the mercy of his local experts who in turn may find themselves influenced by varying degrees of provincialism and self-seeking.

Can one make acceptable decisions in the academic while remaining uninformed regarding the general scholarly direction of the various disciplines and leading an intellectual life that focuses exclusively on issues of management? Perhaps. Can one make decisions that provide academic leadership, that inspire confidence and intellectual excitement? Never. It is a matter of both tone and substance. A campus will expect management, but it will respond only to leadership, and in the academic there can only be one kind of meaningful leadership: intellectual.

Assuming, as has already been done, that our imagined administrator is a person of character, is he prepared to assume office once he has developed his own voice, a persuasive language, and a respectably intense life of the mind? Nearly so. If he has read widely in literature, philosophy, and psychology, he knows a great deal about the nature of man and the spiritual quests that attract him. If he has been a devotee of the fine arts, he knows what exhilaration can come from them; if he knows history and sociology, he has perspective on the present; if he has a well-educated layman's understanding of science and technology, he can appreciate their importance and their limitations; if he has studied political science, he has insight into policymaking. However, an academic administrator will not only lead but manage and often direct a management team whose responsibilities are limited to very specific tasks, say, the operation of an office of financial aid. Consequently, the more extensive the knowledge of the many skills practiced by personnel who form part of a college/university's professional staff and the broader the understanding of all aspects of higher education as a sophisticated enterprise the better. Hence, yes, it is of considerable importance for an academic administrator to understand the consequences on policymaking of centralized

Management Information Systems and aggressive collective bargaining units; to know what elements constitute a well-developed student enrollment and retention program; to have studied effective faculty evaluation systems, strategic staffing plans, and budgetary processes; to have given considerable thought to the significant issues of tenure, academic freedom, and the various patterns of management and governance. All this and a great deal more. Furthermore, it may be nearly as important to have cultivated a judgment that dismisses the simplistic school of academic management that equates lists with uncovered buried treasures: "Fourteen Steps to Handling Angry Faculty Members," "Five Statements to Include in a Letter of Reprimand," "Four Ways to Greet a Systems Analyst."

However, after the higher education seminars and workshops, and summer institutes, however useful, after the exchange at conferences of polished tales in which the narrator always appears wiser, calmer, and wittier than he did at the time of the event, an academic administrator is left alone to practice his art, an art where every major decision is a *vernissage*. Every decision is hung for every critic, trained and untrained, to evaluate and, above all, to interpret. The surface skills, for example, a clever use of the "indirect cost" charge on federal and foundation grants, will be but of passing interest. But what will remain and bear lasting consequences will be the revelation or confirmation of the quality of mind and heart of the decision maker. Proper management is economical; proper management is efficient; but proper management neither inspires nor moves. Proper academic leadership does both, for it not only respects fact, it esteems imagination and honors wisdom.

SELECTED READINGS

Below are works on management and leadership in higher education that have been published in the last 15 years. Some express convictions that are sympathetic in whole or in part to those emphasized in this book; others support styles and views that are nearly diametrically opposed. To each his vision.

Astin, Alexander W., Scherrei, Rita A. *Maximizing Leadership Effectiveness.* San Francisco: Jossey-Bass, 1980.

A 5-year intensive examination of administrative style and its impact on faculty and students in 49 private liberal arts colleges. One of very few studies on the highly complex topic of leadership outcomes. Concludes that an administrator practices an art form and that his works should be viewed and assessed. Advocates a student-oriented management information system.

Baldridge, J. Victor; Curtis, David V.; Ecker, George; Riley, Gary L. *Policy Making and Effective Leadership.* San Francisco: Jossey-Bass, 1978.

A study of decision and governance processes, which describes major developments in academic management. Particularly enlightening on the diversity of faculty autonomy and administrative management styles in institutions ranging from community colleges to research universities.

Baldridge, J. Victor; Tierney, Michael L. *New Approaches to Management.* San Francisco: Jossey-Bass, 1979.

Perhaps the clearest single account of the value for academic administration of the use of MIS (management information systems) and MBO (management by objectives). Many useful suggestions on how to implement such approaches and what traps to avoid. Case studies are analyzed throughout, since the impetus for the study was a request made by the Exxon Education Foundation to determine the impact of changes in management techniques in colleges receiving grants under one of its programs.

Benezet, Louis T.; Katz, Joseph; Magnusson, Frances W. *Style and Substance.* Washington: American Council on Education, 1981.

A report on leadership and the presidency based on data gathered between 1976 and 1979 from statements made by nearly 250 college/university presidents, senior academic officers, faculty, and students at 25 institutions. A useful first chapter, "Perceptions of the Presidency" summarizes the views of some dozen central observers who have researched and studied the same topic.

Bennett, John B. *Managing the Academic Department.* New York: ACE/ Macmillan, 1983.

Descriptions of the practical complexities of administering an academic department from materials originally developed for ACE's Departmental Leadership Institute (DLI). Dozens of short case studies with responses that reveal differing administrative styles maintain an admirable balance by evoking situations concrete enough to identify and evaluate a specific solution and abstract enough to apply to dissimilar institutions.

Blake, Robert R.; Mouton, Jane Srygley; Williams, Martha Shipe. *The Academic Administrator Grid.* San Francisco: Jossey-Bass, 1981.

An adaptation for academic administration of the original grid book, *The Managerial Grid,* published to great popularity in 1964. Readers are taught how to identify their administrative style among the five models described and given reasons to subscribe to 10 principles of managerial behavior. A team approach is viewed as the most effective in handling virtually every task.

Blau, P. M. *The Organization of Academic Work.* New York: Wiley, 1973.

An attempt to relate the performance of faculty and students to administrative structures and degrees of bureaucratization based on data obtained from 115 colleges/universities. Conclusion: excessive bureaucracy has a detrimental effect on teaching and on the integration of the academic venture, but not on research.

Bühler-Miko, Marina. *A Trustee's Guide to Strategic Planning.* Washington: Higher Education Strategic Planning Institute, 1985.

A booklet intended specifically for trustees of colleges/universities, but one which might well be of use to all administrators looking for a concise primer on strategic planning—its concepts and methodologies. The work outlines a step-by-step approach to operational and strategic planning that avoids to the extent that it can the jargon that tends to inflate the difficulty of the topic.

Cohen, Michael D., March, James G. *Leadership and Ambiguity.* New York: McGraw-Hill, 1974.

An analytical report on the American college presidency excluding that of 2-year institutions prepared for the Carnegie Commission on Higher Education. An interpretive essay that combines empirical and theoretical themes in concluding that the position of the chief executive officer in academe is characterized by ambiguity. Its support for a "technology of foolishness" retains, at least for some, its challenge and its attraction. Its call for a systematized theory of management appropriate to campuses described as "organized anarchies" waits to be satisfactorily answered.

Cowley, W. H. *Presidents Professors and Trustees.* San Francisco: Jossey-Bass, 1980.

An examination of the influence, role, and involvement of the many constituent groups in academic governance: administrators, faculty, students, alumni, governing boards, advisory councils, philanthropic foundations, state and federal agencies, and academic associations. The concluding chapter expresses a number of convictions regarding what may be an inevitable tension in attempting to give appropriate recognition to the interdependency of all of the above groups. Cowley, former president of Hamilton and professor at Stanford, died 2 years before the publication of this work, which was edited by Donald T. Williams, Jr.

Davis, Ralph M., ed. *Leadership and Institutional Renewal.* San Francisco: Jossey-Bass, 1985.

One of a series of some 50 paperback source books published under the heading, "New Directions for Higher Education," and the general editorship of Martin Kramer. From the perspective of the firsthand experiences of administrators, faculty, and researchers in a wide range of institutions this volume explores styles of management and leadership in the context of renewal, innovation, and risk taking.

Dressel, Paul L. *Administrative Leadership.* San Francisco: Jossey-Bass, 1981.

An account of an administrator as one who should emphasize the primacy of institutional social responsibilities and ethical value systems that support quality. Not surprisingly, therefore, the strongest and most convincing chapters are the two entitled "Morals, Ethics, and Values in Higher Education" and "Improving Administrative Communication." The author, a professor of university research at Michigan State University for many years, draws on his impressive experience as consultant in analyzing decision making on campuses.

Eble, Kenneth E. *The Art of Administration*. San Francisco: Jossey-Bass, 1978.

A practical guide for academic administrators from one who began his university teaching in 1949 and who has served as a department chair. Its relaxed pace and tone and its homely axioms regarding such matters as delegating authority, communicating, planning and taking risks invariably come to rest upon the support and development of faculty and students.

Farmer, Charles H. *Administrator Evaluation: Concepts, Methods, Cases in Higher Education*. Richmond: Higher Education Leadership and Management Society, 1979.

A compilation and summary of the field of administrative assessment and an identification of the limitations of evaluation systems. Section III describes the practices of administrator evaluation at the University of Tulsa, Austin College, the State University of New York (presidential evaluation), and Furman University. A useful appendix gives a very short description of 28 administrator evaluation programs, which includes the name and address of a person who can provide further information.

Fecher, Roger J., ed. *Applying Corporate Management Strategies*. San Francisco: Jossey-Bass, 1985.

Another in a series of some 50 paperback source books published under the heading, "New Directions for Higher Education," and the general editorship of Martin Kramer. A surface look at a broad range of topics where an application of business principles and practices is deemed not only beneficial to campuses but essential. An open view of the corporate culture is advocated as a means of improving the academy's own.

Fisher, James L. *Power of the Presidency*. New York: ACE/Macmillan, 1984.

An analysis of the different types of power—"coercive, reward, legitimate, expert, and charismatic"—with special emphasis upon the latter as the most powerful in achieving desired ends. A work brim full of convictions and the courage to state them forcefully.

Green, Janice S. et al. *Opportunity in Adversity.* San Francisco: Jossey-Bass, 1985.

A book, containing many case studies, on how colleges can succeed in hard times providing they are blessed with effective leadership. Two chapters are especially convincing: "Leadership: Golden Rules of Practice" by Leon Botstein and "Leaders: Presidents Who Make A Difference" by David Riesman and Sharon Elliott Fuller.

Heller, Jack F. *Increasing Faculty and Administrative Effectiveness.* San Francisco: Jossey-Bass, 1982.

A psychologist's approach to discovering and analyzing the sources of ineffectiveness in a college/university and to instituting strategies for lasting improvement. Detailed examples are used as illustrations of theory throughout and one entire chapter is devoted to a case study of a fruitless attempt to solve the problem of declining enrollment in particular departments in a small institution and the reasons for this lack of success. A section follows a group of administrators as they are taught new and effective action patterns.

Keeton, Morris. *Shared Authority on Campus.* Washington: American Association for Higher Education, 1971.

A report on an effort to understand academic governance through a study of 19 college/university campuses by a committee of prominent faculty and administrators under the directorship of Morris Keeton. The campuses differed widely in climate, size, complexity, location, mission, and autonomy. Recommendations are made as to who should govern and how.

Keller, George. *Academic Strategy.* Baltimore: Johns Hopkins University Press, 1983.

A description of the revolutionary changes in management now taking place on America's campuses and an endorsement of the financial and strategic systems used in business as appropriate tools for coping with academe's contemporary problems. The author, a senior vice-president of Barton-Gillet, an institutional planning and marketing firm, cheers the arrival of the new era and sees the adoption of the latest modes of management as "alert and forward-looking."

Kerr, Clark. *Presidents Make A Difference.* Washington: Association of Governing Boards of Universities and Colleges, 1984.

A report of the Commission on Strengthening Presidential Leadership established by the AGB and based on over 800 interviews with current and past presidents, board members, and executive search consultants among others. Out of respect for the needs and traditions of very diverse institutions, the conclusions take the form of suggestions rather than recommendations, but the central thesis of the study is unequivocal: "Strengthening presidential leadership is one of the most urgent concerns on the agenda of higher education in the United States."

Lahti, Robert E. *Innovative College Management.* San Francisco: Jossey-Bass, 1973.

An endorsement of management by objectives focusing on administration in community colleges. The call is to improve efficiency by applying to the academy managerial techniques taken from profit organizations.

McCarthy, Jane; Ladimer, Irving; Sinefman, Josef P. *Managing Faculty Disputes.* San Francisco: Jossey-Bass, 1984.

A guide to issues, procedures, and practices regarding faculty disputes by the former director of the Center for Mediation in Higher Education at the American Arbitration Association, the former program director of the Research Institute of the American Arbitration Association, and a professor of business law. It distinguishes between approaches recommended for the effective resolution of individual grievances involving, say, promotion and tenure and those dealing with policies such as those governing retrenchment or reorganization. An appendix outlines the grievance procedures followed at Northeastern University, Pace University, and Unity College.

Mayhew, Lewis B. *Surviving the Eighties.* San Francisco: Jossey-Bass, 1979.

A work informed by 30 years of intelligent and perceptive observation of higher education during a time of growth and by the consequent wisdom that might well help those who are responsible for maintaining the integrity of colleges/universities through the 1980s and 1990s, decades of no growth or even decline. The survival strategies are all there: planning for the long term, managing enrollment, improving administrative leadership and faculty performance, controlling program costs, handling crises, and developing a distinctive mission.

Millett, John D. *New Structures of Campus Power*. San Francisco: Jossey-Bass, 1978.

A report of a 2-year study on the changes affecting campus governance following the establishment of campus-wide senates or councils in 30 different colleges/universities. Each case study has its own author: presidents, provosts, deans, professors, and directors of research. The work distinguishes between governance in leading research universities, other universities, and baccalaureate colleges, but emphasizes the imperatives of production management in all institutions regardless of type and views the department as the primary management unit.

Mitroff, Ian I. *Stakeholders of the Organizational Mind*. San Francisco: Jossey-Bass, 1983.

A work whose centrality lies in the conviction that the management of contemporary institutions is the management of complex systems that requires the knowledge of a theory of human behavior in keeping with that complexity. The concept of "stakeholders," external and internal forces that influence decision making, is just such a theory adequate to the task. Archetypes are as apt to inhabit the mind of an academician as the mind of a corporate executive and an understanding of them is most useful in both worlds.

Morris, Van Cleve. *Deaning*. Urbana: University of Illinois Press, 1981.

An experienced individual's perspective of the academic dean as middle-manager. Headings describe accurately the range of issues covered from the administrative temperament to faculty politics to decision making to budgetary and affirmative action matters. An appendix suggests criteria for the evaluation of deans.

Nordvall, Robert C. *Evaluation and Development of Administrators*. Washington: American Association for Higher Education, 1979.

A discussion of the performance assessment of academic administrators excluding chairs of departments that ignores neither the complexities nor the objections surrounding the value of all attempts at formal evaluation in a higher education setting. Various approaches and systems are examined as is the relationship between evaluation results and personnel decisions and development activities. Many references to systems employed both at universities and in business could serve as models that might be profitably adapted to a campus's own individual needs.

Richman, Barry M., Farmer, Richard N. *Leadership, Goals, and Power in Higher Education.* San Francisco: Jossey-Bass, 1974.

An open-systems approach to management in higher education that attempts to steer a course between the position that claims that some management theories are universals that hold for all types of institutions under all conditions and the one that contends that each problem demands its custom-designed managerial decisions. The authors, then business school professors, often compare decision making in academe to decision making in the corporate world. An interesting second chapter is devoted entirely to the mismanagement of a public university with an FTES of 15,000.

Scott, Robert A. *Lords, Squires, and Yeomen: Collegiate Middle Managers and their Organizations.* Washington: American Association for Higher Education, 1978.

Primarily an analysis of the functions, status, and values of academe's middle management based on a search of the literature and data obtained from a questionnaire and structured interviews of more than 200 administrators, faculty, and search committee chairs at 18 colleges/universities of differing size and types. The concluding chapter offers presidents and provosts advice on improving the effectiveness, morale, and accountability of their institutions' middle managers.

Shtogren, John A., ed. *Administrative Development in Higher Education.* Richmond: Higher Education Leadership and Management Society, 1978.

A collection of 16 essays by as many authors on the evaluation and development of college/university administrators from department chairs to presidents. The last chapter, by Jack Lindquist, synthesizes the conclusions, drawn from the experiences recounted in the preceding sections, and offers a list of practical tips. Seemingly everyone agrees that the development of administrators must be planned within each institution's special context and closely linked to institutional development.

INDEX

INDEX